REAL GIRLS GUIDE
to Midlife

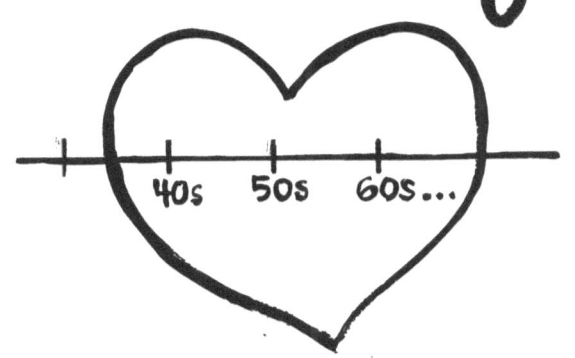

40s   50s   60s...

REAL GIRLS GUIDE —to Midlife

40s 50s 60s...

Hot Takes, True Stories, and Fearless Advice from
Women Who've Lived It & Experts Who Get It

ANGELA BURK

THREE JAYS PRESS

Print Cover & Creative Design by Carrie Drew

Edited by Brad Drew

Typesetting by Zoe Norvell

Published by Three Jays Press

This book is based on personal experience, lived stories, interviews, and publicly available information. Every effort has been made to ensure accuracy at the time of publication. However, the content is provided for general, informational, and storytelling purposes only.

It is not intended as, nor should it be considered, a substitute for medical, mental health, legal, financial, or other professional advice. Always consult qualified professionals regarding your health, well-being, or personal circumstances. The author and publisher make no guarantees and assume no responsibility or liability for any actions taken based on the information presented here.

Certain quotes and contributions appear with permission. In some cases, names, identifying details, and personal characteristics have been changed to protect privacy.

More stories. More truth. Scan to go to realgirlsguide.com, where all the good stuff lives!

To my Aussie Man™, my three boys and my mom,

I am me because of you.

CONTENTS

A REAL GIRLS GUIDE
FOREWORD

Redefining Ambition and Worth: A Love Letter to Women in Midlife

Before we dive headfirst into the glorious mess of midlife, I want to hand the mic to someone who gets it, really gets it. Jenna Richardson is a Certified Menopause Specialist and CEO of Princeton Integrative Health, and she wrote this love letter for every woman who's ever held it all together while falling apart inside. Her words cracked me open in the best way, and I think they'll do the same for you.

Here's what she wrote:

If you're anything like me, you spent years being the dependable one, the capable one, the woman who could handle anything thrown her way without breaking stride.

We learned to measure our worth by what we could carry, by how well we could hold it all together; even when we were bone-tired inside.

I remember my own moment of reckoning. Sitting in my car in a power suit, mascara running down my face, sobbing because everything I'd built looked perfect on the outside but felt hollow on the inside. That moment forced me to stop and ask a question I'd been avoiding: Is this really how I want to keep living my life?

But the beautiful thing about midlife is this, it gives us permission to ask those questions and to pause long enough to hear the answers.

Questions like: What do I want now? Not what I should want. Not what others expect of me. But what truly matters to me.

Success doesn't have to mean grinding ourselves into the ground. It can mean waking up rested. Feeling at home in our bodies. Speaking our truth, even when our voices shake, or people don't like what we have to say. And worth isn't something we have to keep earning by over-functioning, it's something we get to claim simply by being us.

This season of life isn't an ending, it's an opening; a chance to redefine what success, leadership, and joy look like on our own terms.

So, I'm inviting you (no, I'm daring you) to choose ambitions that nourish you, to see your worth as non-negotiable, and to lead from energy and truth, not depletion and performance.

Because, when we choose ourselves, we set a new standard for everyone watching, and that's a legacy worth leaving.

CHAPTER 1

Welcome to the Chaos Club

Approaching midlife felt nothing like I imagined it would.

It started when my ex-husband and I decided to divorce.

After 15 years of marriage and three kids, I had concluded that this was it. Like it or not, the family life we'd built would stick long term.

Turns out, it didn't.

The transition was brutal. It meant letting go of the life I thought I was building and falling straight into the deep end of the unknown. I had no idea what it would look like, how I'd navigate it, or what it would feel like.

The conversation we had with my three boys about that decision is forever etched in my memory. It was gutting. My oldest son, then 12, started to cry. So did my middle son, age 8. The fear in their eyes was worse than the fear in mine. In that moment, I knew that no matter what, I had to fight the fear and do it anyway.

For me. For them. To show them that staying in a relationship rooted in *"Yeah, I could be happier"* was 100% not enough. That despite the fear and the doubt, choosing divorce was critical to my well-being—and what I needed to model for my boys.

Lit the match, burned the script, started over… my way.

It shook every part of the life I'd worked for decades to stabilize: My career. My finances. My sense of security.

Everything I thought I'd built was tied to the life I had with my ex-husband.

I had no idea what divorced life would look like. Sure, my mom divorced my dad, so I knew what it felt like as a kid. But I had no roadmap for my own divorce as a woman at 45, with young boys and a gut-deep need to do better for all of us.

Until that point, my entire identity had been constructed around knowing every next step, calculating every risk, marinating in the worst-case scenario gutter for a bit, and eventually finding my way back to center.

But this? This early midlife shift felt *tectonic*. Like the earth was swallowing me whole. I wasn't just marinating in the gutter—I was *swimming* in it, with my three boys strapped to my back. I had no idea how I'd reach the surface, catch my breath, and power forward.

Deep down, I knew the image I'd created for my "golden years" had exploded.

Now don't get me wrong, not all of midlife was this dark. But some of it? Yeah, dark would be a good descriptor.

For instance: Don't get me started about online dating. I didn't even dip a toe in it. But I had friends who tried to build profiles for me. As a true-crime-doc fan I was convinced I'd end up in the trunk of some stranger's sedan after agreeing to coffee.

No thanks, Tom Hanks, as I like to say.

Besides: What website was I supposed to use? MeetAGoldenGirl.com? (Actually, now that I think about it, that's probably a popular porn category.)

Speaking of porn, here comes the real talk. Somewhere in those post-divorce months I had to admit something to myself: In my entire adult life, I'd probably had a couple of real orgasms. *Maybe.*

The memory was foggy. How, at this point in my life, did I not know what brought me pleasure? Not just in the bedroom—but in partnership, in my life? (Turns out, I like a little soft porn.)

All of this came to a head one night when I had a hilariously awkward fumble with a vibrator. It was basically my first time buying and actually using my new toy—and let's just say it was not the seamless, sexy experience the box promised. First off, I had to remove batteries from the TV remote, then I put them in wrong, couldn't figure out the settings, and the instruction manual? The font was so tiny I had to take a picture with my phone and zoom in like I was decoding top-secret files just to get the thing to turn on.

That was it. I had my moment of *Hell, no*. I was not going to lie down— literally or figuratively—and let all this shit just happen to me. I was going to rise up, figure out that silly vibrator, and embrace the change.

From detonation to reinvention: no map, no manual, just grit, guts, and zero fucks left to give.

That moment lit the fuse. Through my 40s, the changes came in truck-loads. Menopause started creeping in. Gray hairs appeared, and not just on my head. (To which I say: *WTAF?*) My face, neck, and hands sagged just enough that my kids would pinch my skin and ask, "Mom, why does your skin stay like that?"

But inside, something else started to shift.

A slow burn. A sense of urgency.

I still craved stability. It was the reason I'd stayed in my marriage too long and in some jobs longer than I should have, situations that were well past their expiration dates. But now I was sort of waking up. The vibrator incident and the mirror checks added up to one truth: I was in charge now, because of what I'd built for myself.

I was in charge of my finances, my emotions, my future, and my three boys.

Looking back, I remember that I slightly dreaded turning 30 and 40. But something new began to happen as 50 approached: I started feeling fierce. Determined. Ready to burn the old rulebook (a really rigid one I'd written for myself) and to make space for what I really wanted *even when I didn't fully know what I really wanted.*

I had earned this time, at work, at home, in love, and most importantly, with myself. I had to embrace the changes, even the ones I never saw coming. I had to own the fact that I was bold, confident, and had every-thing I needed to thrive. I just had to use it.

That slow burn became a wildfire as I neared my mid-50s. Everything I had done, the choices I had made, the ones I didn't, and the way I wanted to show up for my boys—it was all mine.

This next phase was happening *because* of me. Built *by* me. And *for* me.

I had to show my boys what real grit and hustle look like.

Then I met my partner—a man from Melbourne, Australia—and he took a front-row seat to the many transformations of my 50s.

Expert Q&A: What a Midlife Transition Expert Wants Real Girls™ to Know, featuring Ben Kiker, CMO and Executive Whisperer

Midlife is a lot easier (and less soul-sucking) when you've got community and experts on your side. That's why I've pulled in real-deal pros, people who've coached, counseled, and walked alongside women like us through breakdowns, break-throughs, and bold-ass reinventions. Because let's be real: the best advice, the real permission, and the most honest WTAF-is-happening moments don't come from huge, glossy books or celebrity experts. They come from women like me—Real Girls—who've lived a little, lost a little, laughed a lot, and are still figuring it out as we go.

Meet Ben Kiker, a Clarity Coach and former Silicon Valley CMO who now helps high-achieving women (and some very lucky men) figure out what the hell they want next when the old blueprint stops making sense. He's helped thousands cut through the noise, confront the lies we've been sold about success, and build lives they're actually excited to wake up to. Also, he gives pep talks that feel like both a hug and a slap in the face, which is what we all need once in a while. Here's some sage advice from Ben:

Q: What's the first lie women at midlife need to unlearn to truly move forward?

A: *That they are not enough.*

Q: When a woman says, "I feel stuck," what do you listen for underneath that?

A: *I listen for what follows, because it's usually a story that's not rooted in fact. And that story is generated by what I term the "Insane Thought Generator," and we all have one. Regardless of what you call it, our ITG deals in the manufacture and delivery of unhelpful stories.*

Q: How do you help clients tell the difference between burnout and boredom?

A: *Because one needs rest. The other needs reinvention.*

Q: What's one permission slip you wish every woman over 50 would write herself right now?

A: *If, over the course of a year, anything in your life—a career, a relationship, etc.—depletes you more than it replenishes you, take a very hard look at letting go of that thing.*

Q: What do you say to women who still believe they've 'missed their window'?

A: *Julia Child, Vera Wang, Angela Merkel, Katherine Graham—they are four women who found success after 50. The first brave action is to create the space to allow what is already inside of you to surface.*

Fifty hit like a freight train–one brutally honest reality check after another.

In the early years of our new relationship many things hit at once. I'd leaned into a new life as a single mom, navigated a bucket-list career move that left me fearful for my family's once-solid financial security, and transitioned into full-blown menopause.

My boys were on the brink of becoming hormonal hurricanes themselves. And then, of course, there was the coronavirus pandemic of 2020 which threw life into total chaos.

I was dealing with hormone rage. I didn't recognize it at the time, but now that I do, I feel like I owe everyone in my life an Angela's Apology Tour 2025 T-shirt. I was rediscovering my body, finding my desires, and figuring out my boundaries.

I still *felt* 25 in my head, but sometimes I'd catch a glimpse of myself in the mirror and think, "*Woof. Who's that old lady?*"

I also started to share more about what was happening to me. I was navigating the shifts, reclaiming my body, our voice (me *and* my body), and maybe—finally—my own confidence. And I was doing it with one hard truth in mind: I don't have forever, so I'd better start now.

The other thing I realized around this time was that I'd spent way too long letting other people write my story for me. I'd juggled C-suite boardrooms, faced single-parent madness, and lost count of the red-eye flights from California to Australia I'd taken to keep a long-distance relationship alive.

Amid all that chaos, I realized something: *I have a lot to say at this stage of life.*

And my friend: So do you.

That's why I've designed this book around *our* stories. The crazy ones, the silly ones, the sexy ones.

Our questions. *Our* hot takes.

Your unfiltered feedback shaped every chapter of this book and every topic I'm diving into.

We're going to laugh, cry, cringe, and side-eye our way through the messy highlight reel of midlife. Because let's be real: even the shitshows had something to teach us. I needed every meltdown, every weird body change, every "WTF is my life?" moment to swim through my midlife with grit, wit, and a don't-fuck-with-me kind of confidence.

All of it's in here. And I mean all of it. Because in this book, you'll find:

- Sagging knees and wrinkly elbows
- Mood swings
- Poise Pads as purse staples
- Menopause rage
- Parenting adult kids (without duct-taping your mouth shut—unless that helps?)
- Divorce and dating
- Surviving a household of seven kids across two continents
- Retiring, un-retiring, and redefining ambition post-50
- Finding your own definition of pleasure with sex
- Health curveballs
- The badass joy of still being here

Oh, it's about to get real. But first: a quick Public Service Announcement for all you pushing-50 badasses out there still riding the high of invincibility... Hate to break it to you, but that cape? It starts to fray.

Spoiler: You're not invincible. And shit's about to shift. Buckle up.

A Straight-Talker on Generational Baggage: Meet Charlie Bauman, Licensed Marriage Family Therapist (LMFT) & Family Systems Expert

Charlie Bauman, LMFT, has spent decades unpacking the emotional blueprints we inherit, and the patterns we unknowingly pass on. With a background in counseling psychology and a brutal honesty that cuts through the fluff, he helps women understand why midlife hits so difficult. From mother-wound conditioning to the unseen labor of keeping families afloat, Charlie doesn't just explain the chaos, he gives language to the liberation. His insight into intergenerational roles, codependency, and individuation makes him a truth-teller for every woman ready to burn the old playbook.

The Women's Movement Never Made It To The Kitchen Table

We may have won more rights, more jobs, and louder voices, but when it comes to the household, says Charlie, many of us are still stuck in 1955. The COVID-19 pandemic laid it bare. Women ran Zoom school while managing full-time jobs—or picked up the slack when their partners were out of work.

Why? Because "he doesn't have the patience." Sound familiar? The truth is, family systems are still designed around female-centric emotional labor, and we're not just carrying the diaper bag—we're carrying everyone's emotional load, expectations, and disappointments.

"When everything feels like it's spinning—work, love, body, identity—zoom out. Mindfulness isn't just deep breathing and bubble baths. It's seeing your life from Google Maps view," says Charlie. "It's recognizing that people's behavior isn't always about you—

it's just how they move through the world. The shift? Stop taking it personally. Start seeing the patterns."

Can I get this tattooed somewhere visible, please? Because the number of hours I've wasted wondering what I did wrong when someone else was just living out their own dysfunction is criminal. This is your permission slip to drop the guilt, take the aerial view, and stop editing yourself to fix someone else's script.

Holiday & Event Hell

I asked Charlie: Why do women still shoulder 90% of the work for birthdays, holidays, and celebrations? Because we were trained to, he said. By our mothers, grandmothers, aunties—every woman who came before us and took pride in "doing it all."

Men, meanwhile? Often given a pass, or worse, taught to blame their partners when family life breaks down. The invisible labor of planning, prepping, and pretending everything's fine has become the background music of womanhood.

"At some point, you have to stop managing chaos and start leading your damn life. That means stepping off the hamster wheel of over-functioning and letting other grown-ass adults handle their own mess" says Charlie. "If you're the hardest-working person in every relationship, it's time to STEP OFF."

PREACH.

This is your midlife mic drop. We're not emotional sherpas anymore, carrying everyone else's crap up the mountain while ignoring our own broken ankles. If you're the one doing all the fixing, all the calling, all the caretaking—it's time to pivot from martyr to CEO of your own life.

(continued)

The Good Wife Costume Is Exhausting

Charlie told me this story and it stuck: His wife told him not to wear a ratty shirt to Costco after doing some yard work. He was confused. No one at Costco cares, right? But she wasn't worried about him—she was worried someone might see him and judge her.

Because, for women, a husband's sloppy shirt isn't just sloppy. It's a referendum on her virtue as a wife. We've been taught not to "dirty the nest," no matter how awful the dynamics inside. And that kind of shame? It lives in our bones.

To the 40-year-old cutie who thinks she still has time.

You think 50 is still "someday" away. Cute. You're out here crushing your to-do list, pretending you've got a five-year runway before the real shit starts. But let me tell you—midlife doesn't knock politely. It shows up with hot flashes, disappearing eyebrows, and a full-blown identity crisis in your grocery store parking lot. This isn't a threat. It's a heads-up. It's a love note from the other side. Whatever you've been putting off, do it. Whatever you've been tolerating, stop. Time's moving. So should you:

Hey Girl,

Look, I know you're in denial. But you might as well say it: You're middle-aged.

'Cuz guess what? You're there.

This is a pivotal time. Don't be scared of it. Embrace it. Feel how strong you are and strap in for everything that's coming your way.

Try to remember that whatever you're going through is normal for you.

Find the humor and the sadness, the fear and the anger. Feel all the feels.

Remember that we don't have endless time left. Be bold, take risks, and always bet on yourself.

You're about to slam headfirst into more changes than you can prep for. Some will knock the wind out of you, others will drop you to your knees: It's gonna be messy, humbling, and raw.

Entering midlife doesn't look like it used to. It's OK to face hard truths, to acknowledge what's been missing in your life, to recognize what you want to explore.

Don't wait. Dream. Decide. Do. But make it snappy.

I wish someone had warned me that sometimes all the changes I'd face would hit at once. That the contradictions would be destabilizing. That I'd finally get the chance to do things I'd missed, such as taking my boys to school, only to realize: Maybe they're not as into me as I'm still totally into them. And those unexpected curveballs? They can hurt. A lot.

You'll see and feel some fucked-up things. Your bladder's going to weaken. Your face (and other parts) are going to sag. Things start spreading in places that should probably not spread. You might discover some kinky shit you like—or lose interest in stuff you used to love.

You'll finally stop letting old, narrow, and just plain wrong stories live in your head and guide your every move.

You'll realize how much you actually know and how much value you still bring to everyone around you.

You'll stop asking for permission. Maybe you'll even stop apologizing.

When needed, you'll find the time and space to grieve for your old life, missed opportunities, and things you wish you'd done differently.

But don't stay there too long. Take the shot. You've earned the right.

Want Botox, fillers, or a facelift? Get them.

Want to quit your job and do something entirely different with your life? Now's the time.

Want to move to a different country, break away from a deadened relationship, explore something (or someone) new? Yes!

I'm not judging you, girl. Invest in yourself, do the things you want to do, and if you don't know what you want to do yet, find out what makes you feel like you.

Your friend, Angela

P.S. But for real: Get to it!

Different shitstorms, same emotional forecast: Welcome to your fucking 50s.

It's wild how different life looks for my friends right now compared to what life looks like for me. Yet deep down, we all feel the chaos of midlife.

One friend's husband recently got diagnosed with terminal Stage 4 cancer. She's juggling life as a mom of grown kids (some of whom now have *their* own kids), a demanding career, and an unthinkable reality: a future that might not include her husband.

The weight she carries is immense. It's changing everything about who she is and how she moves through the world.

How can it not?

Forget all this couple's hard work over decades. They built financial safety and security for a future life they imagined together. Now, all that has vanished. It's been replaced by chemo rounds, clinical trials and endless appointments.

Another friend recently left her husband after 30-plus years of marriage. The kids are grown and gone. She'd been easing into retirement, which looked so enviable on social media.

Then: Bam! She discovered he'd been having an affair.

And she was *done.*

No tears. No drama. (Well, I'm sure there was *some* drama.) She was just done.

Hell yes. She said, "Screw comfort, I'm not sticking around just to be someone's second choice." And I respect the hell out of that.

Then there's my powerhouse friend in her mid-50s who's just now hitting menopause. After a recent dinner where she spilled the details about getting a very regular period, I stopped cold to ask: "Wait one second. Do you mean to tell me you can still get pregnant at this age? Woof!"

I have another friend whom I refer to as my fairy godmother of all beauty treatments. She's in the midst of a huge career pivot and recently got a facelift (the first woman I know who's gone that deep). Clearly, she's redefining everything and serving as my guiding light on cosmetic procedures.

Bless her and her doctor.

Another friend is trying to blend a family with a toxic ex in the background, battling migraines, experiencing zero sex drive, and encountering the kind of menopause symptoms someone somewhere in a health class *should have warned us about.*

When she told me that having sex feels like shards of glass, I literally said out loud, "Um, No thanks, Tom Hanks."

As for me? I'm somewhere in the messy middle of all of it.

In the run-up to my 50s, I realized I was in a marriage that was comfortable but lacking. I felt alone so often. I simply couldn't imagine that this feeling was the best I (or my ex) deserved. I wanted to model an amazing relationship, rather than a mediocre one, for my boys. I've weathered the initial big hairy menopause meltdown, a period of intense rage that lasted three years.

Nowadays, I'm in what feels like Round 2. Or maybe Round 3. (It depends on where you rank the act of Googling "How many hot flashes is too many to have in one day?")

It still sucks.

My bladder's staging a leaky rebellion. (Hello? Poise Pads or Depends or Nix? For the love of God, would someone tell me which is the better brand?) Sexy Time Fun Time (aka foolin' around) doesn't always feel so sexy or fun when you're worried about pee dribbles.

Those are some of the downsides. But on the plus side, I'm also clawing back parts of myself that became numb, that I let years of false stories bury—about who I was, what I deserved, how I should behave, what I should tolerate. I'm burning those old narratives down with a blow torch. And so should you.

Underneath it all, there's this fire in me now. You might be feeling it, too.

It's a fierceness, a loud voice that says—no, insists—enough! *"You get to want more. You get to ask for more. You get to take up space, as much of it as you want. You get to be bold."* It's a sense of urgency, really. Like: I can't *not* do these things.

I've always been a little fearful. (OK, maybe *a lot* fearful.) That fear still whispers and lurks. But now there's something even louder: Confidence. A sense of *"Fuck, yes"* that I feel in my body, deep in my bones. I'm carrying myself differently. I'm saying *yes* to things that once would've made me shrink. I'm done waiting for a seat at a table that was never built for me… so I'm building my own table out of hardwood and mettle.

I'm letting people know exactly what I want, what I don't want, and what I'm creating for *me*. This is not someone else's version of what my life is supposed to look like. It's *for* me, *by* me and *because of* me.

Let's be real: This "season" (though I hate that word) is messy. It's gritty. But it's mine.

And I'm simply done asking for permission or begging for forgiveness.

Why So Many Women Don't Spark (Yet)

Because we're still waiting for permission we already have.

Here's the hard truth: So many women don't ignite because they're still stuck in roles that demand they keep everyone else comfortable. They still believe that being liked is safer than being real. They've been trained to ask, "Can I?" instead of "Why the hell not?"

Midlife isn't the end of anything. It's the refusal to keep living someone else's version of you. It's the part where you finally let her out, the Real Girl with the voice, the grit, the fire. Why? Because grit isn't grind. It's staying power. "Grit is passion and perseverance for long-term goals. It's living life like it's a marathon, not a sprint," said Angela Duckworth, in her book *Grit: The Power of Passion and Perseverance.*

Women in midlife know what grit really looks like. It's not working yourself into the ground for approval. It's not white knuckling your way through burnout. It's the quiet power of showing up again, and again, delivering on what matters to you. Grit is the reason you're still standing after divorces, layoffs, death, disappointment, and reinventing yourself for the 17th time. It's not sexy. It's not shiny. It's the steel in our spine. And it's what makes midlife women dangerous in the best way possible.

Sagging knees and other alarming signs you're not 25 anymore.

While I love the new fire and confidence I'm cultivating, I'd be lying if I skipped over the many (many) signs that this stage of life is off kilter. Shit is shifting—*south*, mostly. Things are spreading (wider and weirder), morphing the image I've carried of myself for decades.

I'm strong. I love to work out. I eat pretty well. And I never—*ever*—say no to a spicy margarita.

I've beat cancer twice and still try to take care of this body—flawed, fierce, and held together with SPF and stubbornness. You've probably been to hell and back, too. But still: Some of the stuff that happens to us women at this stage of life? It's just plain *weird*—and honestly, kind of unfair. There are some truly vivid observations women like us make about our aging bodies, or worse yet, the observations that other people oh-so-helpfully make for us.

Let's be real: This can all be jarring, humbling, and sometimes downright depressing.

One of the more brutal parts of this whole Real Girls at midlife thing? It doesn't hit you all at once. It comes in waves: loud, sneaky, occasionally face-slapping waves that remind you, yeah, this is fifty-fucking-five.

I still remember being 20 sitting across from my mom when she dropped this mid-convo bomb like it was nothing: "My knees are sagging." No lead-in. No warning. Just tossed it out there like we were discussing the weather.

I blinked and tilted my head.

"Huh?" I responded.

They were English words, yes. But strung together her comment made zero sense to me at the time.

Sagging knees? What?

Fast forward 20 years.

There I was, in my 40s, looking down at my legs and thinking, "*Oh. My. God. The knees. They're falling.*"

Even better, I recently mentioned this phenomenon over dinner to my much younger sister, who's in her 30s. Later that night, she texted me a photo of her own knees with the caption: "WTAF."

The body horror doesn't end there, friends.

In my early 40s I took my then-9-year-old son (Boy No. 1) with me on an errand to pick up concealer. The sales associate artfully (I use that word liberally) applied it under my eyes. I felt great. Those dark circles and puffy bags? Hidden. She'd nailed it. And so, I bought it. I proceeded to ask my son for his honest opinion about how I looked.

"Well," he began cautiously, "now I can see all the lines and crinkles under your eyes. You should go with the blue circles."

Thanks, kid.

And don't even get me started on my neck.

Or my hands, which are starting to look suspiciously like those of my mom in her 50s—and of my grandma.

And we have the elbows.

Yes, *elbows*.

I have become eerily accurate at guessing a woman's age, plus or minus three years, just by counting elbow wrinkles.

It's a party trick now.

Recently, my 14-year-old (Boy No. 3) chimed in from the passenger seat while we were driving. The sunlight hit my face just right.

"Mom," he said, "this is going to sound gross, but you need to shave your face. You have more hair on it than an overripe peach. Do something. Fast."

Another son, still in his early and innocent years, once asked me why my stomach was so squishy. And another one told me my boobs were big—and long.

Sure, all these things represent a life well lived.

Take the long boobs. They sustained life for my three boys across a span of nearly six years. Now, they're deflated. They're tired. They bought a one-way ticket south and are happily retired, for fuck's sake.

Yet somehow in my head I still feel 25. I still *think* I look 25.

Right up until some cheeky kid cracks wisely or a mirror snaps me out of it. Fill in your own midlife meltdown here; I see you. I feel you. I'm in your corner even if your boobs gave up and relocated south without permission. But don't mistake me for someone who's vain or spends hours analyzing her face in magnified mirrors.

I'm the anti-prepper: wash-and-go curly hair. Five-minute makeup, when or if I even bother. The occasional swipe of lip gloss and the toss of my hair into a ponytail count as effort.

That said, I'm not taking these changes lying down. There are subtle, low-drama ways I'm trying to feel a little more in control, including:

- Occasional facials
- Microneedling (I'm surprisingly into it)
- A little Botox and filler here and there
- Working out (mostly for sanity, but also for strength)
- Also, I've recently started lifting weights (the small, friendly, cute kind)

Here's the truth: I actually feel more comfortable in my skin than I ever have. (I'll have a lot more to say about this in an ensuing chapter.)

Some of that mindset is physical. I finally feel like I'm doing *something* about the southbound slide. Some of it is mental. I'm starting to admit to myself and even to others that I look pretty good for my age. But most of it? It's this new, totally unexpected confidence showing up out of nowhere.

And the real shift is that I no longer feel guilty for feeling good about myself.

It took decades to get here. Decades of criticizing myself for how I looked. For what I weighed. For what I wore.

If I'm honest, I wasn't a great 'keeper' of me in my younger years. I wish I could go back and tell her: *"You're kind of amazing. Please stop wasting so much time picking yourself apart. You're going to age like a badass."*

Tough times don't last, tough women do.

Before we rip the lid off this book, and the beautiful, batshit chapter that is midlife, let's get real: I had some seriously delusional fantasies about what this phase would look like. You probably did, too. And if you're still clutching those dreams like a clearance-rack cashmere sweater, brace yourself.

I fantasized that somehow, after all the chaos, I'd earn a golden ticket to the world's best amusement park. Everything would be calmer, smoother, *easier*.

I thought that after all the shit I'd survived—as a kid, a young adult, a wife, an ex-wife, a mom, a fiancée, a sister, a daughter (you get the drill)—I'd hit some magical pinnacle where the heavy loads would lift and I'd finally coast.

Turns out, not so much.

Life isn't into handing out calm breezes and long beach walks. When you hit midlife, real life's still very much delivering *"What-in-the-actual-fuck is even happening right now?"* karate kicks to the ribcage with a side of whiplash. (And not the cute, hair flip kind, either).

On a regular basis I'm being reminded that some of my old play-books—as a professional, a parent, a partner—are not working anymore. Honestly, a lot of these playbooks need to be burned down. So, here's some truth: you know what you need to do in your own life, and I've got matches with your name on them.

Thought that was all? Guess what: There's grief in this shift, too.

Grief in the fact that I can go days without hearing my son's voices or seeing their faces.

Grief for the quiet gut-punch that I spent years handing over my power, wrapped it up with a bow and gave it to other people's stories about who I was supposed to be. The ones that said stay small, be quiet, and act grateful.

I stood by like a spectator while accepting subpar treatment. Too often as women, and especially as moms, we're conditioned to put everyone else first.

But here's what's different now: I'm not doing that anymore.

I'm finally living the mantras I've been preaching to my boys for years. They include:

- When people show you who they are, believe them.
- Make good choices.
- If you're going to bet on someone, bet on yourself.

Now, in my 50s, I have no tolerance for anything less than truth, intention, and self-respect. I don't have space for people who drain me, try to silence or diminish me, or pretend to love me while treating me like an afterthought.

At this point, for me, the definition of "easy" is changing. It's not about the absence of challenge (though that condition does at times sound dreamy), it's about choosing what—and *who*—is worth the effort, worth my time and worth sharing myself with. It's about finally putting my money where my mouth is and taking radically better care of myself.

Because I've earned that.

And I'm unapologetically reclaiming the choices that definitely should have been mine all along.

So can you.

We've got this. Let's do it together. Starting now.

Real Girls Reboot & Reflections

All right my friend, your turn. At the end of several chapters you'll get a mix of practical tips, Real Girls reframes, and reflection prompts. Plus, the usual dose of humor-laced wisdom (because we all need a laugh while unraveling). The intent is to prompt you with something useful, not just relatable. Now, as some of you flash your AARP card at the door to the Chaos Club, here's three Actionable Tips to kick things off:

Actionable Tip #1:

Create a Chaos Inventory. List every identity, role, and responsibility currently sitting on your shoulders (mom, partner, boss, daughter, emotional support human, etc.). Circle the ones that feel like "shoulds" not choices. That's your starting point.

Actionable Tip #2:

Remember the Real Girls Reframe: Stability is a moving target—so stop blaming yourself for missing it. The goal isn't balance, it's rhythm. And sometimes the rhythm is ugly dancing with your eyes closed. You're still doing it right.

Actionable Tip #3

Don't forget your Real Girls Reflection Prompt. What was your midlife "oh shit" moment? Name the exact second it hit you: *This is not a drill!* Was it a parent's fall? A partner's silence? A doctor's call? Write it down. Then ask yourself: *What did it show me about what I truly value, and what I'm afraid to lose?*

CHAPTER 2

Mirror, Mirror, What The F*ck?

There comes a moment in every woman's life when you catch your reflection or, worse, hear a comment you weren't supposed to hear, and think: *"Who is that?"* or *"Are they talking about me?"*

Aging has a way of sneaking up on you, usually with zero warning and plenty of attitude.

For me it's happened in waves of surprise (and denial).

Remember those stories I told you about the fact that my mom, my sister, and I now share sagging knees? And the one about my son who called me on my lines and crinkles?

Those were horrifying, but then there are the stories I haven't shared. How in my early 50s I spent six months convinced my new "highlights" were sun-kissed blonde. Spoiler: they were gray. Apparently, dark brown hair doesn't spontaneously go blonde at the crown. Who knew?

More recently, during what we'll call my Sexy Time Fun Time reality check, I found myself riding high (literally) when I glanced down and spotted a saggy, wrinkly skin pooch.

A full-on kangaroo pouch.

Nothing like a mid-romp body reveal to kill my vibe.

The common thread? A glaring disconnect between how I *felt* I looked and what mirrors (and innocent bystanders) revealed. Denial? Blindness? Wishful thinking? Probably yes to all.

But here's the aftermath ritual: You need to cue the pep talk: *"Girl, it's fine. You're still cute."*

Then you need an action plan. Most helpful in my experience have been emergency online concealer tutorials, a call to my stylist to tackle the grays (by making them blonde?), and a heroic attempt at sit-ups to "fix" the pooch.

Unfortunately, the pouch isn't just visiting. She's settled in with a long-term lease and zero plans to vacate. And as a bonus? She's made herself real cozy with the front of my thighs. That skin now flaps like an old flag every time I run in shorts.

Oh honey, *yes*—it's like that, and honestly, even more unhinged. Our bodies are shifting, sagging, sprouting surprise hairs, and pulling stunts like they've joined a reality show called "WTF Is Happening Now?"

But let me be real with you:

This chapter isn't about surrender. It's a goddamn rebellion. This is not "learning to age gracefully." This is learning to take your power back, wrinkles, rolls, rogue chin hairs and all.

By the time we wrap up, you'll have a no-holds-barred roadmap for seeing yourself—the real you—underneath all the warped beauty myths and bullshit scripts we've been force-fed for decades.

But first? I need you to unclench. Loosen that grip on what's "appropriate." Because we're about to talk about smearing fish sperm on your face. Yup. You read that right.

Welcome to midlife beauty, baby.

Real Girls Talk: Missy's Mirror Moment

Missy Toy Ozeas, Energy Healer, Intuitive Channel and Creator of the *Become a Money Magnet* workshop, didn't just wake up to a different body—she woke up to a new frequency. "There are days I walk past the mirror and do a double take—not in awe, but in that, 'Wait, what happened to my face?' kind of way," says Missy. The lines are deeper. My arms have a softness I didn't see coming. The body I used to recognize without effort now feels unfamiliar."

But instead of fighting the reflection, she started listening to it. Missy reminds us that aging isn't just a physical shift—it's energetic. It's about presence, sovereignty, and taking up space with something way more magnetic than flawless skin: truth. "Our culture is obsessed with surface beauty. But the energy we move through the world with—grounded, wise, unapologetically real—is stronger than ever."

This is the age of embodiment. Not performance. Not invisibility. The age of not shrinking just because the world is more comfortable when we do. Missy's mirror doesn't lie, and neither does her energy. She's not trying to be admired. She's out here being undeniable. "Aging is as much an energetic shift as it is a physical one."

Sperm, Google searches, and a pap smear from hell.

Since hitting my mid-50s, I've had a parade of "Seriously, what fresh hell is this?" appointments and discoveries that left me questioning my sanity. Turns out I've been waging silent wars I didn't even know I'd enlisted into.

First up: I paid for a salmon sperm facial.

Sperm.

On my face.

My trusted aesthetician (who also occasionally freezes my forehead) convinced me it was the next big thing in collagen stimulation. There I was, lying on a table, microneedle roller in action, getting salmon spawned. As of this writing, I'm only two treatments in. But I *think* it's working. And yet, I still catch myself Googling, *"What other sperm stimulates collagen?"*

Pro tip: always, *always* include "collagen" in that search. Otherwise, you'll free-fall into a black abyss and straight onto a Pornhub niche page.

Think back to the last absolutely bonkers thing you did for the sake of your aging body. I'm not talking spa-day cute! I'm saying "smearing fish DNA on your face while praying to the skincare gods" weird. The kind of choice that makes you stop mid-routine and think: *Is this my life?* Yes. Yes, it is.

And here's the thing: You're doing it on purpose. For you. Because your face, your body, and your badass self deserve more than expired advice from 1997 and a jar of cream from a woman who's never met a wrinkle.

So be kind to yourself. Be weird. Be wildly open. And for the love of God, share what's working with your friends, because some of it will be gold, and some of it will be a cautionary tale best told over a nice bottle of red wine.

Clearly, not every discovery will be pretty. But it'll be real.

A recent gynecologist visit wasn't much better. What was meant to be a routine pap smear morphed into a full-on bladder confession session. I opened up right there in the exam room about the leaking, peeing, urgency, frequency, rogue sneeze accidents, and moments when I'd considered embracing adult pull-ups as a lifestyle choice.

It was less "check-up" and more "group therapy party of one."

My doctor handed me a referral to a urologist and ordered an ultrasound. Other than that? She hit me with the classic *"poor you"* head tilt and served up the medical equivalent of a shrug alongside a few half-hearted "Yeah, it sucks" comments like that's supposed to patch up my unraveling pelvic floor and dignity. Cute try, doc.

But. So. Not. Helpful.

Real Girls Reality Check: Claire's Story

"I went to my doctor because I was gaining weight, I was exhausted, and my sleep sucked. She told me, 'Call me when you haven't had your period for a year.' Then she handed me anti-depressants." Claire did what we've all been told to do: go get answers. Instead, she got brushed off and prescribed pills for her feelings, not her failing hormones.

"When I got frozen shoulder out of nowhere, she sent me to physical therapy. Not one word about perimenopause." This is the unspoken reality for millions of midlife women: dismissed, misdiagnosed, and left to piece together what the hell is happening to our bodies with WebMD and rage-fueled Google searches.

When your body betrays you and the test results say, "Yep, she's cooked."

The ultrasound has been the *highlight* of the great leaking bladder investigation. The irony is that to get scanned, I needed a full bladder—basically, an invitation to disaster when you're already one sneeze away from a Slip 'N Slide situation. Leading up to the appointment, I panicked. I doubled up on the only pads I had in the house (not ideal), wishing I had a pair of "Adult Incontinence Products."

At the appointment, though, my tech was amazing. We laughed about *all* the fucked-up changes. I told her I'd be shocked if she could even *find* my ovaries.

Like: "I spy with my little eye... nothing."

I joked that these scans used to come with baby pics. Now? Just a bladder threatening mutiny and an ovary the size of a pretty well-sucked Tic Tac. Nothing says midlife magic like leaking on your tech while she hunts for body parts that have peaced the fuck out.

The tech wrapped up, and I climbed off the table to put my clothes back on. When I returned to the room, she handed me a printout labeled "Ovary."

Bless her.

I had no clue what size it *should* be at this age. A plum? A grape? A pistachio? Even my mid-50s friend, who I met for dinner afterward, had no idea. What I saw looked like a tiny grain of rice. It was shaped like a rubber duck, oddly enough. I held it up to get a better view.

"Aw," I quipped, "Is it a boy or a girl?"

Later, I googled the ovary size question. (Your online searches are increasingly weird too, right, girl? Please say, yes.) Turns out, in menopause your ovaries shrink to about the size of a small almond. Mine? Nowhere close.

Here's the unvarnished truth: Ovaries get smaller as we age. Once they've run through their supply of follicles, there's no need for them to keep pumping out estrogen and progesterone like they did in our fertile years. So, they downsize, literally, shrinking from almond-sized powerhouses to quiet little pebbles. It's called ovarian atrophy, and it's why post-menopausal ovaries can be hard to spot on an ultrasound. Essentially, they've performed their duties, and instinctively scaled way, way back.

Back to my sad little pebbles. Forget retirement. These little fuckers had *evaporated*. I was just living in another episode of "What's Missing This Week?" starring my reproductive system. But wait... there's more! (If you need to take a lap or scream into a pillow first, I get it. This ride's wild, but I'm not here to torture you. I'm here to walk it with you, heels off, bra flung, dignity optional.) Then, because why stop there, I booked an appointment with an audiologist.

For years, I swore that passing online hearing tests meant I was totally fine. No hearing issues to see here. (Note: There was *a lot* to see and hear, here.) I went into my appointment thinking, *"OK, maybe my right ear's a little off."* Nope. Both ears were off. The doctor cheerfully sent me home with hearing aids to try out.

I broke down in his office, crying hysterically, trying to regain composure, fumbling with my hearing-aid bag while making a beeline to my car. I lasted a grand total of 24 hours before I emotionally tapped out. My son had to return the hearing aids.

I wasn't ready. Not yet.

And if you think *that's* bad, girl, nothing sends me into a midlife tailspin faster than when strangers casually drop beauty secrets that sound like they came from a witch!

The most recent example of this happened on a plane when the woman next to me, a glowing woman in her 60s, shared her beauty secret with me: "Rogaine, for thinning brows and lashes." Ma'am, I am *barely* keeping up with the rogue long dark chin hairs that sprout overnight like weeds. Now you want me to start *activating* growth on my face like a chia pet?

It's true, I'm officially in mourning for my lost lashes. And while micro-blading has helped my brow 'sitch, let me issue a public service announcement: You *will* look like an Angry Bird for about four days.

For the love of God, choose your artist wisely. And whatever you do, don't Google "microblading fails" unless you want to cancel all your plans and question every life choice.

Some of these moments are funny in hindsight.

But in real time? They hit hard. They were little deaths, little waves of grief for the version of myself I thought I'd stay forever. I'm learning, though. Aging is a weird mix of comedy and tragedy.

Sometimes all you can do is laugh, cry, and maybe Google "collagen sperm facials."

Expert Q&A with Nurse Danielle Jenkins: Real Talk on Beauty, Needles and Midlife Glow-Ups

Meet Danielle Jenkins, RN and founder of Fourth Avenue Aesthetics in South Australia. A midlife skin wizard and aesthetic injector, Dani brings heart, humor, and science to aging well. She helps women over 40 reclaim glow, structure, and confidence, without ever chasing trends or erasing character. "The goal isn't perfection, it's presence. We're not chasing a filter. We're helping the world see you again, not just the years," says Dani.

Q: What's the #1 myth women over 50 still believe about injectables or anti-aging treatments?

A: *That it's too late—these treatments only work if you start young. Not true. Skin responds to stimulation at any age. Collagen induction, muscle relaxation, and volume support can all be transformative at midlife and beyond. The real magic happens when women start focusing on themselves again—sometimes for the first time in decades. It's not about looking younger. It's about feeling like yourself again.*

Q: What's one treatment that's overhyped—and one that's absolutely worth the money?

A: *Overhyped: Lip filler for the sake of it. Bigger isn't always better. Worth it: Skin boosters like Profhilo. They retrain your skin to behave younger—no added volume, just glow. Also underrated? Wrinkle relaxers in the lower face and neck. Midlife isn't just about foreheads. Think chin dimples, jaw tension, and marionette lines— small tweaks, big energy shifts.*

Q: Are women over 40 talking about beauty and aging differently now?

A: *Hell yes. Women want to look alive, not 25. There's a confidence revolution happening—but shame still lingers. Wanting to feel seen isn't vanity. Doing something for yourself doesn't mean you're trying to be someone else.*

Q: How do you help clients walk the line between "fresh and glowy" and "frozen and filtered"?
A: *By starting with how they want to feel, not just what they want to fix. "Fresh and confident" is better than "smooth and tight." Treating the face in motion—understanding natural structure and expressions—is everything. Subtle strategy beats overfilling. Less filler. More skin health. Presence over perfection.*

Q: What's one thing you wish every midlife woman knew before booking her first appointment?
A: *It's okay to be nervous. And it's not just about injectables. The best results come from a thoughtful plan—one based on lifestyle, skin quality, and pacing. You're allowed to take your time, ask questions, and change your mind. Find someone who gets your vision, not someone trying to fix you. You're not a project. You're a masterpiece in progress.*

When Botox, lip wax, and boob jobs become your ride-or-dies.

Real Talk: Aging will have you preaching what you once swore you'd never practice: Hello lip filler, goodbye judgment.

You're not flip-flopping. You're adapting. You're doing what works for the body and life you've got now, not the one you had at 25. So, toss the shame, keep the serum, and let your new rules do the talking. I used to think being an adult meant living in black and white with hard rules and clear lines. In my head, I wrote a long list of things I'd *never* do and an equally long list of things I swore I'd *only* do.

Here's another spoiler: Aging is very, very gray (Not blonde, like the color I once convinced myself was sprouting in my dark brown hair). And when things start happening, you act... fast.

Let's break down this beauty crime scene together and trace the evidence back to the version of ourselves we can love. (No bad, out-of-a-box dye jobs required.)

Exhibit A: Lip Waxing Trauma. In my early 30s, I tried a lip wax that left me with what can only be described as a hot dog where my upper lip should have been. Hours before a big night out. Nothing says Date Night Glam quite like a swollen meat stick on your face.

Exhibit B: Botox. I swore it was a hard no. Then, when I was 37, my beauty fairy godmother (aka my very persuasive friend) convinced me Botox should be a "Fuck, yes." One forehead-freeze later, I was in love. I had no regrets. What I *did* have was a smoother forehead and just enough movement left that my boys could still tell when they were in trouble.

Exhibit C: Zoom Touch-Ups. I was late to the game. But once I discovered you could smooth out your face on a Zoom call? I was all IN. Bless the filters, bless them.

Exhibit D: The Boob Job. Once upon a time I had juicy peaches. Then came six years of breastfeeding three kids. Suddenly, I was sporting two deflated balloons. Reality hit the time when my then 5-year-old son observed, "Mom, they're big... and long." He was not wrong. They weren't exactly big, but fuck, they were long. The kind of long that screamed, *"We've officially retired to Florida."*

I'd always said I'd never get a boob job. Until one day I looked in the mirror, sighed, and thought, *"You two must really hate me, huh?"* By my mid-40s, post-divorce, I got tired of mourning the empty space they used to fill, literally and emotionally. So, I brought them back. (Thanks, Dr. K., you're a magician.)

Midlife Body Truths You Shouldn't Have to Google

- Your doctor might not mention perimenopause. You're not crazy.
- Frozen shoulder? Mood swings? Night sweats? All possibly hormonal.
- Peeing when you laugh is common. That doesn't mean it's normal.
- Supplements may or may not work. Your voice always will. Advocate for yourself.
- Looking in the mirror and not recognizing yourself is scary, and normal.

Because pee pads deserve the spotlight, too.

Pee pads are in my purse, and that's not a punchline. It's a strategy.

This isn't graceful aging. This is holding on with both hands and laughing so you don't cry in the grocery store. But I keep trying. Testing. Talking. Loudly.

Because nobody told me how chaotic this life chapter would be, and I sure as hell won't be silent about it now. The body I used to recognize without effort now feels like a borrowed costume. It fits, but it's stretched in weird places, stained with time, and no one gave me a manual.

The beauty lie says we lose value with age. But here's the truth: This is the age of sovereignty. Of self-respect. Of no longer shrinking to be digestible.

My body may not match the filtered, airbrushed version I once chased, but the woman inside it? She's real. She's wise. She doesn't owe anyone pretty, and she isn't disappearing quietly.

Midlife Body Meets Beyoncé Fan:
Maria's Moment

"I didn't know if I was having a hot flash or if the AC was broken at the Austin, TX airport, but I had to stand in front of this giant fan like I was Beyoncé just to survive the heat!" –Maria, 50-ish, retired event strategy badass.

You know it's real when you're publicly performance-cooling in front of strangers, hair blowing like you're in a music video just to survive whatever your hormones are cooking up next.

Maria is just one of millions navigating midlife body mayhem while trying to stay upright, grounded, and visible. She's also a badass who knows that this life chapter isn't just about what's changing on the outside, it's about how we reclaim our presence from the inside out.

Write your own beauty story inspired by
the legends who made you.

When I think about who taught me to feel beautiful, there isn't a singular moment I can point to. There were thousands of small, pivotal ones. Gritty truths revealed in side-eyes, bespoke survival skills, razor sharp looks that said, "stand taller," and lessons wrapped in sarcasm and love from the women who raised me.

Beauty wasn't handed to me. I earned it.

And if you're anything like me, you had to piece some of those lessons together on your own. One hard truth at a time.

Some of them came from my mom. She rarely wore makeup (still doesn't) but could stop a room cold with nothing more than her luminous smile, deep dimples, striking brown eyes, and silver hair that shimmered like spun glass. She carried herself with an ease that said,

"I don't need to try. This is who I am." She never knew or paid attention to the way people looked at her, but I noticed it all.

And then there was my maternal grandmother, Gemma. She had jet-black hair, curves that would make Marilyn Monroe jealous, deep green eyes, and a smile that was sexy and soft all at once. I have a photo of her in a bathing suit posing on a beach in her 20s. She was breathtaking. Effortlessly gorgeous. Sure, she aged. She raised four kids, faced money issues, and cared for 11 grandkids and a few great grands. Yet that image has never left my mind. What strikes me most isn't just how stunning she was but how, like my mom, *she truly had no idea.*

Now there's my Aussie Man who loves me in a way I didn't know was possible. He sees my beauty in places I've spent years criticizing. That butt a high school dumbass declared was "too flat"? My partner would disagree… enthusiastically. Saggy boobs? They get a lot of his attention, and I love each second of it. And those big lips? He sometimes bites them softly when he kisses me, which is a personal fan-favorite move of mine.

He's taught me to see myself through his lens: one that values my strength, my wisdom, and the kind of beauty that only deepens with age.

Growing up, I thought beauty meant having striking features, the kind I saw in the women I admired but never quite saw in myself. Me, girl? I was too busy cataloging my flaws: lips too big, butt too flat, ears that rivaled Dumbo, boobs that took an early retirement package.

Somewhere along the way, we've bought into the lie that beauty is about subtraction—shrink this, hide that, erase the rest.

But here I am now, in my mid-50s, finally beginning to unlearn all that noise. So can you.

Beauty isn't about chasing the 25-year-old version of ourselves, especially not the one who didn't even realize how stunning she was back then. We're not trying to rewind. We haven't lost our edge.

We're owning what's here now and redefining what badass beauty looks like at midlife.

Final Takeaway

I can tell you this: Beauty is certainly *not* about shrinking, hiding, or editing ourselves to be more "acceptable" to anyone else. I have realized beauty was never meant to be measured by what fades. It lives in what stays—the strength, the stories, the unapologetic woman I've become.

So, when that old backhanded compliment shows up—*"You look good for your age"*—it pricks a little, but only for a second. Then I roll my eyes, shake it off, and tell myself: *"Good for my age? Fuck that noise. I just look good. Full stop."*

So do you, babe.

CHAPTER 3

It's Not a Hot Flash, It's a Personality Reboot

The sad reality is that my journey to menopause was long. Like my boobs. You know this by now... And evidently, I haven't scared you away, yet.

Which is good, because we're about to get all ragey.

See, babe, my transition to menopause wasn't smooth. It wasn't cute. And it started creeping in at 37, right when I was trying for Baby No. 3. Thanks to a sweet workplace benefit and one successful IVF round, he joined our family just before I hit 41.

From that point on, everything—my life, my body—was wildly unpredictable.

I was hospitalized twice in six months, once for an infection and another time for a pesky tumor near my uterus. I had debilitatingly heavy periods with gut-wrenching cramps and raging headaches. Some months, I would bleed for 11 days straight. Other months, I'd skip the bleeding altogether.

Back then it was easy to rationalize it all away. I had a demanding job, three kids, a monster daily commute (often 3+ hours roundtrip, not including taxiing my boys all around town) and a body still sustaining my youngest boy's life. I was wrecked. Physically. Emotionally. In so many ways.

I justified the mood swings, the exhaustion, the short fuse. I chalked it up to being overworked, under supported, and stretched beyond thin. I was sick and tired of being sick and tired. But I didn't name it for what it really was.

Fast forward four years. My divorce was finalized. It ended in relative calm after an exhausting marriage. But menopause? Oh, she wasn't done with me yet. My periods came just often enough to tease me that I wasn't through the tunnel.

I'll never forget the day I bled through a tampon, a pad, and my jeans onto the car seat. It was a literal bloodbath.

Hot flash or human torch? Hard to tell. The hot flashes, though? WTAF! They are a *total* mind-fuck. Mine started early, in my late 30s, and hit like a wrecking ball.

I'll never forget the first one:

I was in a meeting with my very tall, confident, assured, fast-on-his-feet-with-a-booming-voice, very executive-level boss, who's now a great friend, thank God. We were talking about launching some big-deal executive customer advisory board when, suddenly, I felt my pant legs getting damp. Like, weirdly wet on the tops of my thighs. Within seconds it was like someone had turned on a faucet inside my body. A wave of sweat rose up from my knees to my neck. I was dripping, full-on desk-puddle sweat.

He cocked his head and asked gently, "Are you okay?"

Um, no sir, I am definitely not OK. I'm liquifying in your office. How is this any kind of OK?

From that point forward, it was game on.

The hot flashes found their ride-or-dies: night sweats. Not the dainty-dewey-cute-glowy kind, either. These were the savage, full body, wake up drenched like I'd napped in a sauna kind.

One night, I hit my menopausal rock bottom. I yanked a towel from the closet, tossed it over my soaked sheets and flopped down like a sloppy, damp, rotisserie chicken. I was done, drained, and too tired to give two shits. And before you ask: No. This was not the good, post-Sexy Time Fun Time wetness. I'm talking massive, swamp-ass sweaty. Just fucking gross.

Around that same time, a younger colleague (humbling in itself) sent me the book *The Wisdom of Menopause* by Dr. Christiane Northrup. It came with a sweet card about how her mom swore by it.

I was horrified. I shoved the giant book on a shelf. I caught glimpses of it over the years but refused to pick it up because doing so felt like admitting defeat.

Here's the real deal, girl: the Big M doesn't knock politely. It kicks the door in, no warning, no RSVP, just a full-blown hormonal home invasion. We don't get to opt out. So, we do what we can with the scraps of info we've got (usually from other women whispering in locker rooms or over wine).

Some days we hold it together with grace and a good bra. Other days? We unravel like a Dollar Store sweater in a wind tunnel, and yeah, sometimes people we love get caught in the blast zone.

When that happens? Don't spiral. Don't shame. Just breathe, own it, and remember: Any woman who's made it this far knows exactly what kind of wild ride you're on. You're not crazy.

You're just in the club now.

Medical Gaslighting: The silent epidemic that's finally getting loud.

You walk into the doctor's office hoping for answers, maybe even a little relief. What you get instead is a pat on the head, a prescription for antidepressants, or worse, dismissed entirely because your labs are "normal" or your symptoms are chalked up to stress, aging, or hysteria (yes, they *still* use that word). Welcome to midlife medical gaslighting. It's not just frustrating, it's dangerous.

And according to a report by the DC Journal, "72% of women say they've experienced medical gaslighting."

Women are told to wait it out, to lose weight, to "calm down." But behind those vague instructions is a complete lack of real care. Hormones get ignored. Patterns get missed. And we're left Googling ourselves into rage because nobody told us the truth: this isn't just midlife, it's a full-body hormonal upheaval, and we deserve better.

The rage years: An apology tour.

I started losing patience everywhere. Let's be real: On a good day, I've got the patience of a gnat. But with menopause, it felt like I'd skipped the "calm and collected" line at birth in favor of the wiry, curly hair one instead. Which really doesn't help much with anything.

No patience at work. At home. With my boys, and with my man.

And what guts me the most now, looking back, is how my kids weren't just bystanders but front-row witnesses to my anger and my rage. They didn't just see the storm. They weathered it. The smallest things would set me off.

A glass in the sink caused instant rage. (It's funny: these days, I'd give anything to see a sink full of dishes. It'd mean all my boys are home again.) My sons' normal brotherly bickering? I'd lose it. I'd slam doors, cry ugly tears, rage hard.

Then, I'd see the confusion and fear in their eyes. I knew I was the cause. I was the one who normally comforted them. Now, I gave them chaos. And they were really young. I can't imagine how unpredictable I must have been. They were probably scared, confused, sad, and mad all at once.

One dinner sticks out like a bruise I gave myself.

I'd taken the boys on a drive to a family favorite Mexican place near the beach. This is the kind of outing I used to live for: long drive, tasty tacos, loud laughter. We sat down and instantly the unraveling began. One didn't want to eat there. Another was whining about who-knows-what. The third just sat in silence like he knew what was coming. Before we could even order, I cracked. I threw down my glass—it didn't shatter, but it was loud enough. I told them to get up. We were leaving.

No food. No family dinner.

Just me falling apart in real time in front of the three people on the planet I love most. The car ride home felt like it stretched across decades. I was fuming but numb, simmering and ashamed all at once. When we got home, I told them to get ready for bed.

"If you're hungry, have cereal," I said.

I had no takers.

They just walked into their rooms: no wrestling, no yelling, no stomping, no last-minute jokes. Just silence. Stoic, heavy silence. And that cut deeper than any slammed door ever could.

The guilt was immediate. But if I'm being brutally honest, in the same breath I felt a strange release. I'd finally said *no* to someone, even if it was the wrong someone. I'd bent myself backward for years—doing, giving, accommodating, sacrificing. All I wanted was one peaceful dinner. Was that too much to ask?

I wonder: Maybe I wasn't the victim that night, maybe *I* was the storm.

Looking back, I can't believe I missed the signs for so long. I'd convinced myself I was dodging the mood-swing bullet because of my slow ride toward menopause. I called it stress. Fatigue. Divorce. Life.

When I hit 47, I finally went to the shelf and pulled down that book, the one from my work friend. I'd been too proud or too scared to open it. But there it was: RAGE, in big bold letters. The topic took up about a third of the book.

I read those chapters in one sitting. And I ugly-cried my way through every single one.

In that moment the hardest part was realizing my three boys had shouldered the brunt of it all. They had no context, no explanation, no reference point. All they saw was their mom, normally their steady rock and their safe place, shifting into someone else entirely.

I can't help but wonder: Who did they really see when they looked at me back then?

And how much of her do they still carry?

The hormonal hijacking of midlife.

Here's a little story about Cara I like to call: "The Doctor Said What?"

Honestly, all things considered, Cara did everything right. She showed up at her doctor's office because she was gaining weight, she was exhausted, and she couldn't sleep. Instead of support, she got shrugged off and handed antidepressants.

"Oh, just call when you haven't had your period for a year," her doctor told her—like that's the magical timestamp for when women become worth treating again. She also developed frozen shoulder—suddenly, painfully, and without explanation. Her doctor sent her to physical therapy. No mention of perimenopause. No hormone tests. Just another woman in midlife told, essentially, "It's all in your head."

Some women crash into perimenopause like it's a hormonal car wreck. Real Girl Maggie described it like waking up in a stranger's body. Her sleep, her thoughts, her feelings, her ability to exercise, everything changed. Nothing felt familiar anymore. And no one around her seemed to get just how upside-down her world had become.

It wasn't until she got on MHT (Menopausal Hormone Therapy, thanks to a brilliant, progressive doctor in Mexico) that things started to click back into place. She said it was like losing her mind, then finding her "me" again. Maggie's custom compound cream became the anchor she never knew she needed. And it wasn't just about estrogen. It was about getting her *self* back.

Here's the part that makes her furious: so many of her friends, smart, strong, accomplished women, have been pushed into surgeries for frozen shoulder, all while no one mentioned that estrogen loss could be the root cause. She's seen it happen over and over again. The silence around it? Infuriating. The number of women being gaslit by their own healthcare providers? Frozen shoulder, hot rage.

Fucking unacceptable.

The Hormone Replacement Therapy Hustle

For Maggie, healing didn't come in a neatly labeled bottle from her local pharmacy. It came with grit, resourcefulness, and a shipping workaround that would make a smuggler blush.

Since her U.S. address can't receive direct shipments, she pays her mom's landscaper to cross the border, pick up her custom-compounded HRT cream in Mexico, and ship it to her from California. Meanwhile, her 87-year-old mother (on HRT for 36 years) is a living, thriving reminder of what's possible when women have access to real care.

(continued)

Her daily hormone blend includes:

- Bioidentical Estradiol
- Progesterone
- Pregnenolone
- Testosterone
- DHEA

It's not just a regimen—it's a lifeline. One that actually works. One she had to fight for.

And that's just one part of her return-to-self journey. In early 2024, she tried something most doctors won't put on a prescription pad: a guided therapeutic mushroom session. Maggie called it life-altering. She said she met God—and God was stunning.

(*Note:* **HRT** *stands for Hormone Replacement Therapy, a treatment that provides the body with hormones that are no longer being produced in sufficient amounts, most commonly during menopause.* **MHT** *stands for Menopausal Hormone Therapy, another term often used in place of HRT, especially in medical contexts, to describe the same approach to easing menopausal symptoms and supporting long-term health. Call it HRT or MHT—either way, it's basically giving your body back the good stuff it decided to quit making.*)

Not every path to healing is mainstream. But it doesn't have to be. Whether it's bioidenticals or bio-spiritual breakthroughs, what matters is that it *works*. That it brings you back to yourself. That it reminds you that you are still *in there*—and more powerful than ever.

Enter Cris Amato, MSN, APN, RNFA and Founder of Grace Concierge, who delivers functional, personalized care for midlife wellness. She works with midlife women to untangle the mess of misinformation, bad science, and outdated care protocols.

Cris confirms what Maggie and so many of us already knew from lived experiences:

- Hormonal chaos is real and reversible.
- The now controversial 2002 Women's Health Initiative (WHI) study that said HRT led to multiple health issues in postmenopausal women? According to some experts, the study was flawed, misinterpreted and fear-inducing, causing lasting damage to women across the globe. (Source: UCLAHealth.org)
- The right treatment is personal. Think advanced testing, bioidentical hormones, and lifestyle shifts.
- Most importantly? Women don't need to suffer quietly.

Tears, triggers, and the truth: Why I cry like it's my superpower.

The honest truth? I'm a big crier. It doesn't matter whether I'm angry, hungry, frustrated, sad, or happy. I cry. Always have and likely always will.

My dad used to dare or demand me *not* to cry in certain situations which, shocker, made me cry even more.

I've cried at my kids' school, at work, at the doctor's office. (One good cry happened after a cancer diagnosis, so that was totally fair. And a second cry happened after I learned I needed *two* hearing aids which, again, also fair.)

Then there was that episode in the plumbing aisle at Lowe's—yes, *the home improvement store*. That day, I'd already been to Lowe's multiple times tackling a bunch of fixes to a house we'd just moved into. It was pouring rain outside and my shoes and pants were soaked.

I was desperate for help, standing next to a sweet old man who was just trying his best to help me find a new hose to replace the one that turned my laundry room into a splash zone. The man wasn't getting paid nearly enough to deal with me and my menopause-fueled meltdown, but there we were, the two of us and my flood of emotions.

I've cried with my boys. Not often, but it has happened. Still does.

These days, I'm currently deep into Wave 2 (or is it 3?) of menopause mayhem and I've definitely teared up mid-argument with the kids. It usually happens when I'm worn down from arguing the same point for the 87th time or I've hit my limit on the sass someone's giving me like it's their job.

I'd found my person in comedian Tina Fey, who once quipped: "*Some people say, 'Never let them see you cry.' I say, if you're so mad you could just cry, then cry. It terrifies everyone.*" She's not wrong. And the looks I get during an ugly cry? People are confused, panicked, scared shitless. My opinion? They *should* be.

I remember once when my Aussie Man and I were in California. We'd just moved into the second home I'd bought post-divorce, because nothing says emotional stability like a more expensive mortgage payment and a dozen or so home improvement projects. We'd done some light upgrades, cosmetic stuff, but I was already in that familiar fear spiral, mentally tallying every dollar and feeling one Home Depot (or Lowe's, because they *love* me there) run away from a breakdown.

As we began to settle in, he started to insist we needed blinds for all the windows. And sure, I wanted to cover the windows, too. (I'm not feral, for fuck's sake.) But I'd just replaced every single window, and I needed a minute to emotionally recover. He pushed: "Let's just have someone come out and measure."

Fine, I thought. *Whatever. Let's do the thing.*

The guy showed up, did his measuring magic and dropped the number: $2,500. Not tragic or catastrophic. But in that moment, in front of both, I cracked. I walked down the hall and called out to my man: "Can you come here please?" Then, I burst into tears, sobbing, borderline hyperventilating.

It was one of but not the very first time he'd seen me like that. His face said it all.

"Is she short-circuiting? Do I reboot her?"

As I tried to explain myself between gasps, I managed to get it out: It wasn't about the blinds. It was the pace, the pressure, the zero control over yet another decision I wasn't ready to make.

Instead of hugging me or whispering, "We've got this," he looked me dead in the eye and said, "I don't know what's going on, but you need to talk to someone." Honestly? "Calm down" would've hit better than that. Instead, I got the emotional equivalent of, "*Bitch, you need help.*"

He wasn't wrong. But still, maybe lead with a hug, babe. Not the mental health referral.

Fast forward seven years to the present, and these moments still happen, usually about money. I get anxious. I cry. I get loud. But now, I see it coming. I hear myself.

If I'm spiraling hard, if I taste metal in my mouth, if I sweat (not the hot-flash kind), and if my chest gets heavy, I know what's happening. And my man has learned to engage with me in those moments more productively. His "you need to see someone" retort is now an inside joke between the two of us.

Expert Q&A with Dr. Carol Queen:
Real Talk on midlife hormones, libido,
and the WTF of wanting.

Midlife doesn't just fuck with your periods, it fucks with your libido, your confidence, your sleep and your definition of "normal." So, we went to Dr. Carol Queen, longtime Sex Educator and Staff Sexologist at Good Vibes, to get straight-up answers to the questions we whisper in group texts and scream in therapy. Guess what? You're not broken, you're evolving.

(continued)

Q: So many women in midlife feel like desire packed its bags and left with their estrogen. What's actually happening—and how do we get the spark back without faking it or forcing it?

A: *Anyone who didn't realize hormones were important learns it at midlife! As our so-called "sex hormones" shift, libido and ease of orgasm (if they were ever easy) can seem to vanish. But it's not just estrogen—it's everything: sleep disruption, hot flashes, mood swings, and energy crashes. Add in dryness, pain, and less sensation? Yep, sex can feel more like a chore than a thrill.*

And if your partner's attitude sucks? Well, desire doesn't exactly thrive in resentment.

But let's be clear: Our culture didn't prepare us for any of this. Most women have had zero mentoring around perimenopause or long-term sexual evolution. We don't expect our sex lives to change—so when they do, we feel confused and ashamed instead of informed and empowered.

Q: What myths should women over 50 finally burn to the ground?
A:

- *That sex has to look one way.*
- *That it's only real if it's penis-in-vagina.*
- *That if you're with "The One," sex should always work.*
- *That there's nothing you can do when it stops feeling good.*
- *That sexy equals being wanted—instead of being turned on by your own life.*

Most sexual distress comes from believing in "one normal." It's BS. There's no single way to be intimate, and pretending there is? That's what kills desire faster than any hormone shift.

Q: What do you say to the woman who still wants intimacy, but her body doesn't cooperate—painful sex, dryness, or just straight-up disconnect?

A: *First: get a doctor who knows menopause. Many don't. Ask about hormone therapy—it can be a game-changer. And please, know that painful sex isn't just something to "deal with." It's a sign. Your body is asking for care, new turn-ons, and a redefinition of what pleasure means. Explore with yourself or a partner (if they're willing). Figure out your new normal. Use lube. Ditch the scripts. Penetration isn't the gold standard. It never was.*

Q: How does redefining sexual pleasure in midlife become a tool for reclaiming personal power—not just in the bedroom, but in life?

A: *When you step up for your pleasure, you step into your power. You communicate better. You take your needs seriously. You prioritize your body, your comfort, your growth. You stop waiting for someone to tell you you're desirable—and become the one doing the choosing. That ripples everywhere.*

Q: If a woman says, "I don't even know what I want anymore," where should she start—body, heart, or vibrator?

A: *Yes. All three. Start where it feels safe. Breathe. Touch without performance. Let your body guide you without expectation. Your heart may need to grieve, your mind may need to reset, and your vibrator? It might just be your new compass. And here's the kicker: the longer we go without sex, the harder it is to start again—especially post-menopause. Solo pleasure isn't just fun, it's functional. It keeps your sensual self awake. Sex isn't something you "graduate from." It's something you get to keep rewriting, again and again.*

My past doesn't get to narrate my future.

I've changed a lot emotionally over the past five years. Not in some big, explosive, action-movie-climax kind of way, but in a slow, steady burn. The kind of change that works its way in quietly, until one day you wake up and realize: *I don't carry shit the same anymore.*

In a way, it feels like this radical self-possession.

It's a don't-fuck-with-me sense of calm I feel more often than not. A no-bullshit baseline that cuts through the noise I spent years suffocating from and drowning in. These days, many of my old patterns have short-circuited.

My old doubts aren't completely running my show anymore. What's left is this new brand of confidence that's earned, sharpened, and fully mine. I've learned I don't owe anyone an apology for, or an explanation about, how I feel, what I do, or why I need what I need. I've stopped rationalizing and silencing my emotions just to keep the peace. That old loop still kicks in sometimes, however: I'll feel something, question whether I'm "allowed" to feel it, then start negotiating with myself.

But now? I interrupt it. I cut the cord. I speak up. I say what's on my mind, how it hits me, and what I need moving forward.

I've also gotten better at setting boundaries. Not in a dramatic slam-the-door kind of way (though let's be honest, I still keep that hot little move in my back pocket) but in a "here's what I expect, here's what I won't tolerate" kind of way. I spent decades sitting quietly, hoping people would just *know* better, *do* better.

Now? I use my voice.

But it's not just about being louder. I've also become softer too, more empathetic, more reflective. I can't think back to my "ragey mom" era without wincing. There's guilt and, yeah, regret. I hate how out of control I felt in my own body. I didn't recognize myself some days.

And my boys? They were seated in the front row. They saw it all: the exhaustion, the short fuse, the spiral. Their world was already upside down after the divorce, and I wasn't always the anchor they needed. That's a hard truth to sit with. But I do.

Because here's what I know now: No one is the perfect mom. No one is steady 100% of the time. That's a myth. And honestly, some of my grit was born out of those messy moments with my own parents. Maybe, just maybe, those moments are shaping my sons into more compassionate, resilient humans, too.

Now when guilt creeps in, and it still does, I remind myself that I can't rewrite the past. But I *can* choose how I show up now. When I screw up, I name it. I explain it. I say sorry when it's needed. And I hope that teaches my boys, and all our combined brood, how to do the same. How to own their messes without shame.

Maybe I'm even helping them develop their own Spidey senses. Because hormones? They're like fine wine or ripe French cheese: they age, they evolve, and they get funkier.

To my sons especially, for the lessons we've learned together—the good, the messy, and everything in between—I say thank you.

And yeah, you're welcome.

Expert Q&A with Cris Amato:
CEO Of Grace Concierge, Nurse Practitioner
And Midlife Hormone Whisperer

You're not crazy. You're not broken. And you're definitely not alone. Cris Amato has worked with hundreds of women who show up foggy, frazzled, and fed up. She's here to remind us— midlife changes are real, fixable, and no, "it's just stress" isn't a medical diagnosis.

Q: When should we raise the hormonal red flag?
A: *It's not "just aging" if you suddenly feel anxious, avoid friends, or*

can't remember words you used to toss around with ease. Cris sees it all the time: women who've lost interest in their partners, their passions, and their spark. Brain fog, palpitations, introversion, irritability— these are signs your hormones may be hijacking your life. A tiny boost of testosterone or estrogen has literally changed women's careers, confidence, and energy overnight.

Q: About that WHI study that scared everyone off HRT...

A: *Cris is done letting outdated research run women's lives. She arms patients with real data, new studies, and tools to challenge dismissive doctors. Her motto? Education is power. If your doctor tells you to "just meditate and wait it out," come back with receipts—and options.*

Q: Labs vs. "It's all in your head"

A: *Yes, Cris loves a good lab test. But she also listens. Really listens. Because sometimes the issue isn't estrogen—it's low iron or tanked vitamin D. Doctors who don't believe in testing? Cris calls BS. She says: "Get the baseline, get the full picture, and get your damn support."*

Q: How about metabolism, menopause and that sneaky sugar trap?

A: *Midlife insulin resistance is real. Cris keeps it simple: Ditch hidden sugars (even that "healthy" creamer or sneaky-sweet bread) and notice how quickly your bloat, brain fog, and belly poof shift. She recommends starting with one change, then building from there. Oh, and if you're serious? Try a glucose monitor. One client found out rice cakes were her blood sugar saboteur. Boom, life changed.*

Q: Vitality looks different. Here's how to claim yours.

A: *If you walk into Cris's practice saying, "I don't feel like myself anymore," here's what she'll tell you: "You're not crazy. You're not alone. And this is fixable." Whether your path is HRT, better nutrition, pelvic floor therapy or all of the above, she's not here to push, she's here to partner. The goal? Fall back in love with your current self, do not* *chase the ghost of your 30-year-old body. Also, question: Why do men get Viagra? And who exactly do you think they're having sex with?*

Q: Now let's talk sex (because someone should).
A: *Dryness, pain, and low libido aren't "just part of aging"—and Cris isn't having it. Her go-tos?*

- *Vaginal estrogen (a dream for pain and dryness)*
- *Pelvic therapy (fixes incontinence and bad sex)*
- *A little testosterone (if your doc won't prescribe it, find a new one)*

If I were a room...

If my personality were a room, I'd have door locks that turn only *from the inside*. Those weren't there before. I used to leave the door to the real me wide open, hoping people would just treat the space with care. Now? I decide who comes in, how long they stay, and whether they get a seat or just a hallway glance.

There's a "No More Bullshit" welcome mat, a full-length mirror that doesn't lie, and a shelf filled with notebooks and journals I used to be scared to write in. The lighting is bright and brutally honest, but it's still flattering. I've stopped softening things to make them more palatable. This room glows. Nothing is too flashy and it's all very cute.

My room is a mix of soft things and hard surfaces. There's a cozy couch for crying because yep, I cry a lot. My same old ugly, joyful, exhausted, enraged tears show up for all my feels. But right next to that is a steel-plated table with a sign that reads: "My silence doesn't mean you've won."

Across from that is a weathered, oversized Restoration Hardware-style chair, one that's solid, grounded, built to hold the weight of big things. It gives *"Yeah, go ahead and sit down, but don't get too comfortable"* vibes.

Also, there's a sledgehammer leaning on the wall in the corner just in case something needs breaking. On a small table is a wooden plaque that reads: "Choose your approach wisely!"

I tossed out the old cedar chest where I once buried my feelings, stuffed swallowed truths, and packed worn-out apologies. In its place is a heavy steel workbench, scuffed and solid, where I lay things out and work in plain sight.

I don't shrink back to keep the room quiet anymore. My boundaries aren't walls; they're reinforced doors and warning signs. Above the door leading into my room is a flashing neon sign, one with the words: "Enter with care."

Lastly, but maybe most importantly, is a rusted-out fire alarm behind cracked glass situated on the far wall. It's labeled, "Pull When Ready." And it's always ready.

The urgency and steadiness I feel now are impossible to ignore. I no longer agonize about the right moment or the perfect words. I've got shit to say, moves to make, and a life to finish building—now, with my own hands.

And I'm fucking done waiting.

It's Not Selfish, It's Survival:
Midlife moments with Charlie Bauman, LMFT

Why do so many women feel guilt, not power, when they finally start prioritizing themselves in midlife?

Because we've been trained not to, according to our favorite LMFT and Therapist, Charlie Bauman (you remember him from Chapter 1), who breaks it down like this: From the moment we're old enough to hold a doll or pour juice for someone else we're taught that our value lives in our service. We're socialized to be the glue. The cheerleader. The one who remembers the birthdays, books the pediatrician, and makes peace over the Thanksgiving table. And God forbid we drop the ball or, gasp, say no.

Then when we finally hit midlife and the fog lifts just enough to say, *"Wait... what do I need?"* the guilt hits like a hormone-fueled freight train. Because wanting something for ourselves still feels like a betrayal of all we've been told to be.

Charlie explains it like this: "Men are raised on the Three A's: autonomy, assertiveness, achievement. Women? We get the Three S's: subordinate, self-sacrificing, and smile pretty. And when we start reaching for those A's? That friction? That shame? That's the sound of centuries of social expectations cracking wide open. Guilt is forgetting to pick someone up at the airport. Shame is believing you're a bad person for even having needs."

Midlife isn't just a hormone rollercoaster, it's a full-blown identity reckoning. A reboot. A rebellion. Not because we're broken but because we're finally remembering who we were before the world told us who to be.

From survival to radical self-possession and self-compassion.

I've carried guilt for a long time. The kind that lingers even after the apology. The kind that creeps in during quiet moments. I've replayed all the ways I wish I'd done it differently.

Especially as a mom.

Especially after the divorce.

I've spent years beating myself up for the times I was short, sharp or simply too depleted to be the steady, calm presence I wanted to be.

I thought being accountable meant punishing myself, carrying the weight, not letting myself off the hook.

If I kept the guilt close to the surface, I reasoned, maybe it would mean I cared enough. But, there wasn't one particular dramatic situation or tearful breakthrough. It happened slowly, over many quiet moments strung together across years of looking back.

I'd be folding laundry, and my mind would flash back to a scene I wished I could rewrite. Driving alone I'd remember a moment when one of my boys needed calm and, as per usual in my most ragey years, I gave him chaos instead. These memories didn't just visit. They stayed, lingered, haunted me. And for a long time, I let them.

But eventually something shifted. I started sitting with those memories instead of trying to outrun them. I let myself feel the ache of what I didn't get right, the regret of not being the mom they needed in the hardest years.

And in that space, without anyone else telling me it was OK, I finally said it to myself:

You didn't know. You were trying. You're doing better now. Let yourself move forward.

So, I wrote it down.

To My Boys,

Everything good in me lives in you. I know I hurt you sometimes. I know I scared you sometimes. I know I wasn't always the mom you needed. And I'm sorry. For the yelling. The silence. The times I chose tasks over connection. The nights I pushed through instead of slowing down. The moments when my own pain got so loud it drowned everything else out.

I'm sorry for the confusion, for the distance, for the fact that you had to sit in it without really understanding what was happening. I'm sorry that my unraveling became part of your childhood.

I can't change that. I wish I could. But I hope you know I've never stopped trying to make it right. I haven't always shown up as the version of me you deserve, and I know that. And I know there are times you feel like you're coming in last, buried beneath everything I'm carrying for everyone else.

But I also know you've helped me become a stronger, bolder, fiercer version of myself than I've ever been. I love you for that. And I'm sorry for the times my fear, my silence and rage took over. I know it wasn't easy to be on the other side of it.

It wasn't until I hit 50, and then some, that I finally began to loosen my grip on the mistakes I'd replayed for years.

Not to erase them. Not to pretend they didn't happen. But to stop carrying them around like a life sentence and start moving forward with grace.

Because the woman I am now doesn't wear shame as proof of how much she cares. She owns her truth, says sorry when it matters, feels every single thing and still moves.

I'm still learning. Still doing the work. Still showing up for the hard parts. But I'm done waiting for permission to let myself heal.

That's not weakness.

That's me walking out of my own wreckage.

Love, Mom

CHAPTER 4

Parenting After You're Supposed to Be Done

Looking back, the signs were there. Some were subtle, others were loud and duct-taped.

I'm in the twilight zone of parenting now. Two of my kids are over 18 and one is still at home. I'm not managing screen time anymore. I'm managing silence, distance and the emotional landmines of letting go.

I should have realized it during California's COVID-19 lockdown when my two most feral sons wanted to box, as in Mike Tyson box. I wrapped their hands in T-shirts and duct tape and sent them outside with one rule: No faces, no ER visits.

DEFCON 1 parenting at its finest.

No one tells you how brutal this shift is.

One minute you're the center of their universe—the sun around which everything orbits. The next? You're just static in the background. They hear you, but they're not really listening. Until, of course, you get *17 missed calls* at 1 a.m. because their car broke down while they were out with friends. Suddenly you're not just relevant again, you're their emotional punching bag.

Let me be crystal clear: This happened to me.

I was sound asleep, blissfully unaware. And in the span of five minutes, I missed those 17 calls. When I finally answered I stayed on the phone until the tow truck came, until they made it safely home. I did what I always do: I showed up. But during that hourlong call I absorbed it all—the panic, the frustration, the short temper, the "Why the fuck didn't you answer?" tone. Like I somehow *caused* the breakdown. As if I had personally sabotaged the car.

(By the way, *I bought that car*. You're welcome, kid.)

The part I hate to admit is that I muzzled myself with the same duct tape over my mouth that I'd used to fashion boxing gloves. I swallowed my rage. I didn't say the thing I wanted to scream: *Don't fucking talk to me like that!* I didn't match the energy, didn't hang up, didn't make it worse. I didn't want to start a war at 1 a.m.

But make no mistake, I was *fuming*. Pissed. Deep-in-my-bones pissed. And that anger sat in me like a live wire. Because while I was trying to be the calm and supportive soft place to land, I was also silently screaming *I deserve better than this*.

And you'd better believe the next day, that kid and I had a *chat*.

Now, here's the deal: Just because I'm always there for them doesn't mean I'm disposable. Just because I'm the safe one doesn't mean I'm the one you get to unload on. I will *always* show up, but I will not be your emotional trash can.

Spoiler: Parenting older kids isn't the exhale people make it out to be, that idea is total bullshit. When they were little, I worried about scraped knees and broccoli. Now, I worry about bar fights, heartbreak, student debt, and existential dread.

The stakes are higher, the consequences are bigger, and my control? Gone.

What's wild is how different they all are. I used to lump them together as "The Boys." One strategy fits all. Wrong. Hilariously, epically wrong.

My oldest is basically me with better sneakers. He tolerates my lists and reminder texts. Sometimes he even says thanks.

My middle son? Every time I try to "help" it's like I'm dousing him in emotional bug spray. Once, after a very gentle nudge about school, he ghosted me for a week. I cried daily. Stared at my phone like it owed me an apology. That silence? It wasn't rejection—it was a boundary. But it gutted me.

That moment tore me open. He was stepping into his life. I was clinging to mine.

Now I watch each of them build futures that look nothing like the ones I imagined. And that's the hardest part. I'd always pictured steady jobs, degrees, neat little timelines. Instead? They're taking gap years. Applying to fashion school. Pursuing creative work. Taking slow, winding paths that make my Type A soul want to scream.

What I'm learning is that their lives were never mine to script.

Today, I'm cheering instead of steering. I'm holding space instead of holding on. I'm putting the fiction aside and showing up for the reality, even when it doesn't follow my plotline. That means loving the kid who's thriving in fashion. The second one who's still figuring it out. And the third who just wants space (the one who sometimes only texts "OK").

Because if I keep gripping onto the stories I wrote for them, I'll miss the lives they're living. And I don't want to be the mom who makes them feel like they have to earn my pride.

I want to be the one who shows up—fully, fiercely, and without flinching—for the real versions of them.

When You're Supposed to Be Done Parenting, But You're Still on Deck

Many of us think midlife is supposed to come with a final whistle: your kids launch and you get to tap out of parenthood. Except for so many of us, that whistle never blew. Adult kids call. Old roles drag on. Identity crashes the party. With all that in mind, here's expert-backed advice with attitude to help you shift from "mom manager" to emotionally badass co-pilot:

1. Lead with curious AF empathy

Therapist Julia Samuel, in The Times UK, notes when your adult kid calls you out for being emotionally distant, the answer isn't defense—it's curiosity. Dial down the drama and ask, "'Help me understand what you needed?' Let listening replace defending. Magnify understanding, not ego."

2. Fire your inner middle manager and hire a consultant self instead

Julie Lythcott-Haims, Author of *How to Raise an Adult*, reminds us: Being a mom to grown kids means mental micromanagement doesn't belong anymore. You're no longer the boss of their life, you're the wise guide who pops into their inbox when invited. Giving unsolicited advice? That's old-fuckin-school.

3. Set kickass boundaries (without guilt)

In midlife, you need emotional space more than ever, define what you'll tolerate (money, time, drama) and communicate it calmly. Doing so isn't harsh, it's adulting with respect, for them and for yourself.

4. Expect grief, but don't check out of joy

Letting go of your parenting identity hits harder than you'd think. It's not about losing your kids, it's about losing the daily caretaking. Naming that grief opens the path to quiet joy and reclaimed boundaries.

5. Trust them to screw up and grow

Tess Brigham, a Family Systems Therapist cited by The Hartford, advises you to let your kids stumble and learn, that's how resilience is built. Jumping in every time? That just fosters dependency. Let them have their mess.

My most epic parenting fails (a.k.a. growth moments in disguise).

Looking back, I can't point to many big, dramatic public failures or huge moments with strangers as witnesses. But there were (and still are) times when I unravel in front of the people I'm supposed to protect.

At that time not only was I dealing with this massive life change, but the menopause meltdowns were hitting hard and fast. I was full of rage and fear, and I had no idea how to hold any of it.

I shared in the previous chapter the story of the night when I broke, that doomed trip to the Mexican restaurant. I wasn't the safe place my boys needed. I was the storm they had to weather. A slammed glass, three silent boys, and a brutal realization later, I recognized I wasn't just missing the mark, I was the wreckage.

Fast forward in time to what was probably the third (or fourth… or eighth) breakup between my son and his first girlfriend. Here again, I felt the familiar burn of helpless, protective rage take over my body like a wildfire.

But first, let's pause so I can share a quick glimpse into my overall mothering mindset.

When my kids are hurt my instinct isn't calm or reason, it's vengeance. Mafia-style. If you come for my kid, I will come for you. I've never acted on it, obviously, but the urge to destroy anything that wounds them is visceral. Bone-deep. Primal. It's probably why my middle son once casually told me I reminded him of Beth Dutton, a character from the TV show, *Yellowstone*. At the time I'd only seen one episode.

"Why?" I asked.

"Because she'll do anything to protect her family," he said. "That's you."

After finishing the series and seeing Beth's felony track record stack up, I told him we might need some light mother-son therapy. This is also why my kids keep sending me memes of some over-the-top, badass mom moment where she loses her mind in defense of her child. And every time, they tag it: "This is you."

They're not wrong.

The Shock of Silence:
What happens when they go?

No one really tells you what happens when your kids grow up. There's no roadmap for the quiet grief, the shifting identity, or the strange space between being needed and being released.

One day you're in the thick of it—carpools, curfews, snack drawer invasions—and the next, you're staring at a spotless house that feels haunted by who you used to be.

Molly Carroll, Therapist and Host of the *Cracking Open* podcast, knows this heartbreak intimately. After dropping her son at college, she describes walking into her house and feeling like her heart had been ripped out. "Not to be dramatic," she says, "but I felt as if I'd lost a limb." She'd published books, delivered TED Talks, and built a business. She'd even met the friggen Dalai Lama. But none of it prepared her for the identity fracture that came with losing her most defining role: being a full-time, deeply-available mom.

Cassie echoes this multi-layered grief. After years of caregiving for her mother with Alzheimer's and raising her sons on her own, she hit an emotional wall in the transition to empty nesting. One son boomeranged home after health issues, the other is still job-searching. "The bounce-back," she says, "makes it a rollercoaster."

On the other hand, Leigh found surprising ease once her daughter left for college. Their home had been an emotional minefield during the Covid-19 pandemic, but the distance created space for both of them to breathe. Leigh converted her daughter's room into an office, and her daughter flourished. "I'm so proud of her independence," she writes. "And I'm proud of myself for letting go, so she could grow."

And then there's Candice Suarez, a cancer survivor who lost part of her tongue in treatment but found her voice in the process. She founded *Season of Flight*, a community for empty-nest moms learning to grieve and fly. As a life coach for teens and their moms, she helps women let go and rediscover themselves. Candice, who built *Season of Flight* to hold this sacred transition, says, "It's not about moving on. It's about moving forward—with eyes wide open, heart cracked but still beating."

In the end, this life chapter isn't just about letting go, it's about what happens to *you* in the absence. Because midlife mothering isn't the end, it's the beginning of a radical rewrite.

(continued)

When parenting gets more complicated, not less.

It's not always a clean break, unfortunately. Sometimes the grief is layered with guilt, estrangement or emotional boundary whiplash.

Dotty, a business owner over 55, shared this devastating reality: Her 28-year-old daughter cut her off completely, blaming her for a less-than-perfect childhood. She blocked Dotty from contact, and Dotty is now grieving the living—her daughter and the grandchild she'll never know. "This generation doesn't want parents," she says. "They want people to blame."

Christine Dickson, a Transformational Mentor, realized she was too available to her adult daughter—answering every venting call, offering too much advice, and slowly becoming drained by it. When she finally set boundaries and shifted their dynamic, their relationship deepened. It didn't happen overnight, but it happened.

Lorraine's daughter is a world-traveling firefighter and ski patroller. Not incidentally, Lorraine has weathered her child's near-death calls, brutal breakups, and full-on trauma therapy after a hiking accident her daughter survived. "Parenting adult kids is not for the faint of heart," she says. "It's lonely, layered, and full of love. And while my kids are grown, I'm still growing too."

Dr. Nivedita Nayak, a Clinical Psychologist, calls this period one of "silent grief and invisible reinvention." She works with women who are estranged, sidelined, or stuck in a cycle of caretaking adult kids who still haven't launched. "I love him, but I don't want to keep being his landing pad," one of her clients whispered, and then wept.

This is the part of the story we don't talk about enough. The part where motherhood and martyrdom get untangled.

Rewriting The Role:
From manager to consultant.

"When your kids are young, you're their caretaker. As they grow you become a manager. But after 18? You're a consultant. You don't send invoices, but you also don't do the work for them anymore," says Author and Podcaster, Sarah Wendell. "You offer wisdom, not micro-management."

To be sure, Sarah's motherhood framework should be plastered across a billboard in massive lettering: Caretaker, Manager, Consultant.

Kerri Acheson, a mom and educator, reinforces this shift. Her adult sons know she's there for them in a pinch, but she's had to learn when to step in and when to stay out. When one son floundered in college, she intervened *with his permission.* That part matters.

Remember Lorraine's daredevil daughter? She abruptly moved across the country at age 18, and never stopped adventuring, which took its toll: "I'm her emotional emergency contact from 8000 miles away. Last year, she fell 20 feet off a cliff while hiking. She walked away. I didn't, I needed EMDR therapy just to process it."

Parenting from a distance means learning to hold space for their freedom without collapsing under your own fear. Leah, a marketing strategist, may have put it best when she said: "I wish someone would ask who I am without a child attached to my name."

(continued)

Tools For Reinvention:
Process, reflect, and reset.

Alexis McCray, Ed. S and LPC, suggests identity mapping and grief journaling as two powerful tools. Writing unsent letters to your child can help, as does reflecting on who you were and who you want to be. Letting the waves of grief come, not to drown you, but to cleanse the space you need for becoming.

"No one really tells you what happens when your kids grow up, there's no roadmap for the quiet grief, the shifting identity, or the strange space between being needed and being released," says Alexis.

Which begs the question: What if we stopped asking how to fix the gap between us and our grown kids? What if we filled that gap with ourselves?

This isn't the end of the parenting story.

It's the start of your own.

Finally, Molly Carroll leaves us with this brilliant summation: "The journey of letting go isn't about losing who we were as mothers—it's about reclaiming who we are as women."

Back to the wildfire called Angela's Havoc...

There I was, in Australia. It was early morning in the Southern Hemisphere when my phone rang. My son was on the other end–crying, gutted, heartbroken, humiliated, and angry. Another breakup call. I wanted to climb through the phone and pull him into my arms. I wanted to wrap myself around his pain and make it stop. I also wanted to strangle that girl. I'm talkin' full-blown felony-assault-level rage.

But more than anything, I wanted to scream: *What the actual fuck are you doing, going back to her again? Why are you letting someone treat you like this is all you deserve?*

That last part hit me like a self-inflicted knife wound.

Because at that moment I realized I wasn't just angry at her—I was terrified that this was somehow my legacy. That my son (maybe *all* of them?) had learned this kind of tolerance from me. From years of watching me shrink. Stay quiet. Carry emotional blame that wasn't mine. Sit in a marriage where I made myself small to keep the peace.

The things my son said on that call, the way he blamed himself, the questions he raised, wondering what was wrong with *him*. They weren't new to me. They were echoes. I'd said those things, too, at a different time, in a different relationship.

Now, I was watching my son carry the same fucking weight I'd spent years trying to set down. Did I model this? Did I miss the signs? Could I have stopped this spiral?

But here's the beautiful, breath-stealing part.

A few hours later he called me again. He was calmer. Grounded. Different. Without me prompting or nudging him, he said: "I think I need to talk to someone. I need help figuring out why I feel this way." That came out of *his* mouth. Not mine.

My son, at 21, came back to me not as the broken boy on the other end of the 5 a.m. call, but as a man beginning to make better choices. Not because I told him to. Not because I fixed it.

But because *he* wanted something more for himself.

Real Girls Talk: What happens if you don't shift?

- Adult kids emotionally shut down—or treat you like an ATM.
- Resentment bubbles under your control and guilt.
- Your identity stays stuck in outdated parenting roles.

Another Letter To My Boys.

To My Dear Sons,

Let me say loud, clear, and dead real, guys: I'm still your mom.

Not the diaper-changing, crust-cutting, park-sitting version. (Although I'd give anything for one more afternoon of sticky fingers, and hours more of "Mommy, look!"). No, now I'm the late-night-texting, overthinking, try-not-to-call-twice-in-a-row (but 9 times out of 10, I do this anyway) mom.

The one who still pays for your phone bill yet gets ghosted when I call.

Love that for me.

This version of motherhood? It doesn't come with milestone charts or cute check-lists. There's no handbook for parenting grown-ass kids. There's no script for how to hold space when you're also holding back tears. There's no guide for when to step in, when to shut up, or when to just quietly Venmo you gas money and say, "Drive safe."

But here's what I know: I haven't stopped showing up. I won't stop showing up.

Being your mom now means watching you stumble and not rushing in to fix it. It means holding my breath through your heartbreaks, your confusion, your detours—knowing I can't shield you anymore. Even when you're building lives I don't get to orchestrate. Even when your pain looks eerily like mine. I know I shouldn't.

It means swallowing my panic and saying, "I trust you," even when I don't fully trust the world you're walking into. And yeah, sometimes I bite my tongue so hard it bleeds. Sometimes, I give advice you didn't ask for. Sometimes, I take your silence way too personally. But that's what this part of parenting is: It's fucking messy, and brutal, and more beautiful in ways I never saw coming.

Because that's what this phase looks like.

It means sitting on my hands when you make choices that scare me. It means cheering for dreams I didn't see coming. It means forgiving myself, over and over, for the ways I got it wrong, especially when you were too young to know what I was carrying.

It means I still keep the fridge stocked with your favorite snacks. Send "just checking in" texts I know will likely be left on "read." Pray like it's my full-time job that you are safe and secure. Show up when you call at 1 a.m. because your car won't start and you're pissed at the world and taking it out on me.

It means I have to sit with the truth that sometimes I was the chaos instead of the calm. That I've had to grow up right alongside you.

I'm still your mom. And that doesn't mean I hover (well, not as much). It means I hold space and boundaries. I also hold back, even when I want to control the situation, and I hold you up when you forget who you are.

I don't always get it right. But I will never stop trying to love you better—not just as my kids, but as the men you're becoming. Because no matter how far you go or how grown you get, I'm still your mom.

And you're still my heart, walking around in this wild, messy world.

Love, Mom

CHAPTER 5

You, Me, Our Baggage (and Our Luggage)

I didn't know what love really looked like in my 20s. In my 30s, maybe I had a slightly sharper lens—but not by much. Back then, love felt like something that hurt more than it healed. It was full of conditions, quiet resentment, and emotional isolation. Or worse, it came with the paralyzing numbness of being stuck. I loved my kids with everything I had. My family, too.

But inside my marriage? I was lonely as hell.

I didn't have the words for it, but I knew it wasn't enduring or built to last. And I knew I didn't want my boys growing up thinking this was the best a loving partnership could offer. They didn't know the whole picture, but they saw enough: the tension, the emotional distance, the way we slowly stopped reaching for each other.

That version of love? I wasn't going to let that be their model. I had to show them something else even if that something was just me, on my own but not disappearing. I used to think love meant compatibility. Shared routines. Someone who remembered your drink order. But now in my mid-50s, after everything I've learned, unlearned, blown up, and rebuilt, I know better.

Love isn't about companionship. It's about capacity.

The capacity to get uncomfortable. To sit in the hard conversations. To hold your ground *and* your partner's hand at the same time. To trust someone enough to show them every messy part of you and not flinch when they stay.

In my case, maybe the wildest thing is that I found that kind of love 8,000 miles away, on another fucking continent. My partner lives in Australia. I live in California. My Aussie Man and I don't have a Hallmark "Meet Cute" moment. We met through our work, we were friends first, held many common interests, a connection followed, and then love sparked in its mysterious and ethereal way. But somehow, across oceans, time zones, and a whole lot of chaos, we've built something solid. Real. No bullshit. No pretending.

I'd be lying if I said there weren't some memorable knock-down talks. And like most partnerships, oh yes, we've hit some emotional walls.

But what we've also done is show up for the work. We've unpacked baggage from past marriages. Faced the triggers. Screwed up the boundaries and had to fix them (or, in some cases, built them from the ground up with concrete and steel).

The distance didn't weaken us. If anything it made our connection stronger because we *had* to communicate. We choose each other every single day, even when it isn't convenient or simple. Which it is not.

Sure, there are moments I miss the everyday things. Like having someone here when my water heater exploded. Or when I called a plumber because I forgot Australian faucets, located in the Southern Hemisphere, run hot in the opposite direction. (Thanks, Boy No. 3, for "fixing" that by turning the knob in our kitchen the other way.)

I miss the closeness, the reach-over-and-touch-you ease, the cooking together, the early morning coffees in bed. I miss having someone to help handle the shit that comes up. But I'll take this kind of deep, deliberate connection over proximity without intimacy any day.

And when it comes to the messy stuff like exes, blended-family boundaries, and old wounds that flare up, we've stumbled hard. But we've also called it out. Named it. Dealt with it. That's the difference. That's the growth. And that's the kind of love I never would've known how to hold onto in my 30s.

Fuck, I couldn't have conceived of it back then.

So yeah, it's weird. It's not traditional. But it's real. It's ours. And it's built on capacity, not comfort. It's a choice we both keep making, even when it's hard. Especially when it's hard. And it's hard a lot.

Love at this stage isn't a fairy tale. It's not sunsets and synchronized heartbeats. It's more like two grown-ass adults showing up, beaten down, battle-scarred, baggage in hand, ready to build something that doesn't need Instagram approval or a how-to guide.

It's not cute candlelight dinners, it's "Did you book the flight?" and "Did I leave my black bra in Australia again?" This isn't soft-focus, perfect-lighting romance. This love is full-volume, full-contact, and full-effort. It's midnight check-ins, long-haul flights, mismatched schedules, and still making it work because you *want* to.

Love after 50 isn't about finding your other half—honestly, love should not be this at any age.

It's about being whole on your own and choosing someone who matches your chaos, your clarity, and your capacity to show the hell up. Sometimes, you have to torch the old script, grab a stiff drink, look life dead in the eye and say: "Fuck the ending someone else wrote. This one's mine."

When Selfhood And Partnership Collide: Real Girls experts on midlife love, labor and letting go.

Why is midlife love so frustratingly hard?

Because it demands reinvention at the exact same time life demands stability. We're evolving while holding down long-term marriages, aging parents, grown-but-not-gone kids, demanding careers, and unraveling hormones. We're expected to stay grateful—for the life we built—while quietly wondering: *Is this it?*

Lauren, a 50-ish, powerhouse executive and mother of three, put it this way:

"I didn't expect the roles to become so clearly defined and yet still feel so unsatisfying. Garbage is his. Dinner is mine, but so too is the emotional load. As our kids became adults, the issues got harder—work, relationships, identity. He once helped with midnight feedings. Now, I'm carrying the heavier emotional weight alone. And that lift? It's heavier than ever."

Remember Charlie Bauman, our favorite LMFT with more than 15 years of experience working with women and couples? Well, he sees this dissonance play out daily: "Many women want to step into their own identity, but feel trapped—financially, emotionally, relationally. They fear conflict. They feel selfish for wanting more. And they're terrified of what will happen if they actually say what they need out loud."

When Lauren lost her father—her anchor—grief collided with success: "I'd hit a professional high but still felt hollow. I've learned to tie my choices to gratitude, because they are choices. But sometimes, it still feels like something's missing."

And then there's *intimacy*—not just sex but being seen. Again, Lauren's version is achingly honest:

"I wish I could say I have what I'm about to describe. I don't, not consistently. Intimacy now looks like being considered. Filling my gas tank. Picking up flowers. Clearing the clutter—not because I asked, but because you noticed. Feeling supported without spelling it out."

Dr. Nick Bach, PsyD., Psychologist and Marriage Counselor, says this about asking for what you want: "Love at this stage isn't a reboot—it's a rewrite. Women want to be seen, but don't always feel safe asking for what they need. The ones who do? They're not needy—they're inviting their partners to know them."

And when it comes to sex? Utkala Maringanti, LMFT Associate and Sex Therapist, reframes it entirely: "Many women are learning—some for the first time—how to ask what they want. Post-menopause can be sexually liberating, but only if you stop waiting to be fixed and start asking to be fulfilled."

In the end, what's Lauren's advice to her younger self? "Demand more. Early and often. Don't accept less—because less snowballs. Digging yourself out takes a big fucking shovel."

Love, lube and the TSA: The Real Girls rules of long-distance romance at midlife.

Romance in midlife, especially with a partner living on another continent, isn't always flowers and flirty emojis (but it can be). It's scheduling, stress, and holding your shit together with emotional duct tape.

When it's Week 12 of living the solo life (which is about as long as we go between in-person visits), desperately Googling "TSA rules on vibrators" because you've officially gone from *I miss him* to *I might hump this pillow* doesn't really sound all that crazy.

The distance also does another wild thing: It scrambles your memory like an old-school Etch A Sketch. It's very odd, I forget his annoying shit.

Like how he can turn a simple hand wash into a full-blown water park situation on the bathroom counter. He, in turn, forgets that I treat closet doors like suggestion boxes, almost shut, but never quite.

Cute, right? Until it's not.

Reintegration after time apart isn't just about syncing time zones. It's re-learning how to share space with someone whose presence has been pixelated for weeks.

As for me, I dive right into something I call the "Yes/No Game" in which I answer a question and he has to guess whether my "yes" actually means "no." (Only, I forget to tell him it's a game, and then I get mad when he loses.) Or if my "I'm fine" actually means "I'm fine" or *Proceed at your own fucking risk, mate.*" (Fact: It's the latter 99% of the time.) It's a delicate dance, there is no doubt.

Early on, long-distance love felt like a soft-core porn scene with decent lighting. Every visit was hot, dramatic, and intense. We'd forget there were bills, exes, and Wi-Fi issues waiting at home.

I still remember meeting in Rome, our flights synced like foreplay, passports practically throbbing. And let's just say the hotel sexcapade? Unforgettable. Cute little spot, paper-thin walls, headboard banging like a drum solo, and then boom: a next-morning buffet showdown with the sweet older lady who *definitely* heard every moan, gasp, and "don't stop." Bon appétit, signora!

But now? Real life shows up in airport sweats with jet lag, no shower for at least a day, lost luggage and a long-ass to-do list.

Re-entry can be a shitshow. Like clockwork, the universe throws a grenade or two right before we're supposed to reunite. Because nothing says, "Welcome back, baby," like emotional whiplash and a calendar that looks like a war zone.

I've had a trip derailed by retinal detachment (yep, no flying for 12 weeks). And yet, that man dropped everything and flew across the world to help me recover. Another time? He injured his ankle right before a multi-city airport sprint. I ended up sweating through three airports pushing him in a wheelchair while half-laughing, half-plotting whether I should let go on a downhill just for the adrenaline rush. (I didn't!)

This is romance at midlife. There are fewer rose petals, more "let's fuck fast before the kid walks in," forehead kisses mid-meltdown (usually mine), and a sex bag tucked in the nightstand on both continents. It's messy, it's maddening, it's occasionally wildly inappropriate (sorry not sorry, kids–you were warned).

And honestly? It's still kind of hot.

Inner Child, Outer Chaos: Loving with luggage in midlife.

Every relationship in midlife—whether it's a 30-year marriage, a second shot, or a solo chapter—comes with a carry-on full of emo-tional inheritance. Trauma. People-pleasing. Perfectionism. Sex shame.

Missy Toy Ozeas, the Energy Intuitive we met earlier, puts it bluntly: "Midlife intimacy isn't just better communication. It's healing the scared kid inside you who learned love meant self-sacrifice." She had to stop over-functioning in her own marriage. Her healing came from telling her inner child: You don't have to earn love anymore. You're already enough.

And what about the nervous system's role? "Midlife anxiety in relationships isn't always about trust—it's about decades of nervous system dysregulation," explains Holly Gedwed, LPC-Associate. "You're not just learning to speak up—you're rewiring your body's stress response."

According to Viviana McGovern, EMDR-Certified Therapist, she sees women panic at healthy love because they're still wired for abandonment. "Trauma resolution helps them feel safe not because someone saved them—but because they stopped seeing love as a threat," she says.

Then there is female codependency, a specialty of Dr. Ann Kra-jewski: "The shift happens," she says, "when a woman stops becoming who she thinks her partner wants and starts becoming herself." Ross Hackerson, LMFT, calls it relationship archaeology: "It's the process of digging through years of adaptation to uncover your original desires."

"If I meet a man who compliments where I'm going, great," says Cassie, a single mother of boys. "And if not, that's fine, too." That's not bitterness. That's radical self-possession, because when your nervous system and your inner child both feel safe? You stop re-enacting the past. And start building love that feels like *liberation*.

This is radical midlife intimacy. Not fairy tales. Not fixing.

Just truth.

From Silicon Valley to an Italian Villa: How we built a blended family across two continents.

Let's set aside life as a couple for a minute because love is one thing, but raising seven kids across multiple continents comes with zero manual (I have three, my Aussie Man has four). That's where the real story begins.

And when you and your partner live on opposite sides of the world, you don't get the luxury of proximity. You get Wi-Fi, time zones, and a whole lot of screen time. FaceTime. Zoom calls. Letters. (Yes, like actual hand-written, paper ones.)

Somehow, we've patched together a relationship built on pixels and per-sistence: one call, one text, one love note at a time. And then, we started making it real.

Meeting each other's kids? That part was really beautiful. Nerve-wrack-ing, emotional, totally surreal. But beautiful. They were curious, kind, and open in ways that still move me.

Meeting the exes? Yeah, not so much. My ex made his stance crystal clear by straight-up ignoring my Aussie Man the first time they met. No handshake. No eye contact. Just pure, icy shade.

My man's ex? Well, she spent years casually reminding me she'd been there first with stories that began, "Remember when we …" These encounters often ended with me wanting to flip a table. But that noise eventually faded as we worked hard to build something real.

Something ours alone.

Once, my boys visited Australia for an entire month. I've made multiple trips with my youngest. My man and I have crossed the Pacific Ocean more times than fucken Captain Cook—him to California, me to Melbourne.

We visit his daughter and her wife in Colorado whenever we can. We've juggled schedules, school calendars, custody arrangements, and jobs to make space for each other. But in 2019, we did something huge—we got *all seven kids* (plus one partner) in one place for the first (and, so far, the only) time about three years after we met.

We chose Italy: Two weeks, one villa, ten humans, two rental cars. And one shot at seeing if this whole chaotic family experiment could work.

Surprisingly, it did.

There were late-night swims, dance parties, soccer (they call it *calcio* in Italy) in the dark, and a competition involving who could eat the most pizza.

Meltdowns happened (some adult, mostly kid). A couple people caught the flu. There were personality flare-ups and drama. But there was also laughter, connection, and a shared rhythm that somehow started to feel like family.

One night after dinner, my man and I slipped away to the bedroom, each with a glass of wine. The kids were being loud. Then someone spilled something. Another knocked on the door. We looked at each other and didn't even have to say it out loud.

This is our circus. These are our monkeys.

And we wouldn't trade it.

That trip confirmed what we'd suspected but hadn't quite dared to believe: that what we'd built a world away from each other, with six kids still under our roofs, wasn't a fantasy. It was working. We didn't just *blend* a family. We built one across borders, baggage, exes, and all.

And we're still building it, every day.

When The Marriage Mirror Cracks:
The midlife crossroads dressed up as chaos.

What do you say to the woman who wakes up at midlife, looks around, and doesn't recognize her life—or her marriage? The truth? It might be a crisis or it might be the most honest invitation of her life.

Charlie Bauman, LMFT, sees this all the time: "A woman might start by questioning her relationship," he says, "but she's really awakening to herself." Many women in long-term partnerships are the glue. They remember birthdays, manage holidays, clean up emotional messes. That is, until they're done being adhesive. Not out of bitterness—out of *resurrection*.

And yet, these same women often have partners who haven't built emotional lives outside the marriage. When the kids move out, when the wife starts changing, many husbands panic. Resent. Retreat. Charlie's truth? "Alone isn't the enemy. Abandoning yourself to avoid being alone is."

Real Talk, real toys, and really bad angles.

‹ CATEGORY 5 SHITSTORM WARNING: To my kids and family, this is your cue to slam the laptop shut, toss this book across the room, and pretend this chapter never existed. ›

Real Talk: When you're not with your partner all the time, Sexy Time Fun Time requires creativity… and a few deeply questionable camera angles. Between all the flirty emojis, marathon FaceTimes, endless Zoom dates, and shared-book bonding, we've also become proud (and mildly shameless) curators of NSFW exchanges.

My photography skills are average at best, but let's just say my man has a solid collection of panty pics snapped in wildly unsexy places: cars, closets and, yes, the occasional locked office bathroom. (You're welcome, babe.)

But before I could confidently fire off a crotch shot mid-Zoom call or snap a cheeky panty pic from a hotel bathroom, I had to figure out what actually *works* for me.

Suffice it to say, in my 20s and 30s my relationship with self-pleasure and orgasms were nonexistent. Like, full-blown no-fly zones. A crotch cobweb convention. Masturbation and me? We were basically estranged relatives: third cousins, twice removed, who met once at a wedding and never spoke again. I'd heard of it, maybe gave it a lazy try once, then ghosted it like a bad Hinge date. For decades.

My previous relationships were straight-up vanilla, and not the good kind with little flecks of real vanilla bean mixed in. We're talking plain, no sauce, no swirl, barely a nibble of actual pleasure. There was zero curiosity from them and not nearly enough demand from me—because how the hell do you ask for something you don't even know you want?

I didn't explore. Didn't push. Didn't play. I just kind of showed up. And so did they. Barely.

Now? Whole new era.

Post-divorce me met her first vibrator and immediately got baptized in the church of the detachable shower head—and babe, I've been a devout member ever since. I launched into my 40s like a one-woman science experiment: a lot of trial, a lot more error, accidental power surges, missed spots, and one overworked vibrator that tapped out mid-session like, "Girl, I did my best."

I had to learn what worked, where, how, and with what level of force before I could even *think* about sending a crotch shot without flinching.

Then came my Aussie Man (pun not intended). For the first time I had a partner who didn't just want to get me off, he wanted to understand what made me tick, twitch, moan, and beg for more. No shame. No shortcuts. Just real-deal curiosity, communication, and the kind of mutual pleasure that should honestly come with a warning label.

We've fumbled, we've laughed, we've broken a headboard. And somewhere in all that sweaty, explicit trial and error, I found what I never had before: a sex life that's mine and fully turned the fuck on.

What I've learned? I like being on top. Shower sex used to be a cute yes, but is a firmer *No thanks, Tom Hanks* these days. I'm open to most things (and most of my places are open for business). A little porn never hurts. I'm pro-oral, giving and receiving. I can do light kink, but I draw the line at anything requiring a safe word or clean-up crew.

And threesomes? Hot in theory, until you're knee-deep in body parts, bad angles, and someone who catches feelings. Sounds less like a fantasy and more like a group project that ends in tears, a yeast infection, and a *Judge Judy* rerun.

The truth is I fumbled my way through those early exploration years. I wasn't always graceful or articulate. But the desire was real, and for the first time, I had someone who gave a fuck about what *I* wanted. Who didn't just want to get off but wanted to understand what got *me* off.

That kind of care? That kind of partnership? It's legendary.

Final Takeaway

It took me hitting my 50s to say this shit out loud—not just to myself, but in writing. (Sorry, kids, if you missed the disclaimer at the top.) And to my dear neighbors? If you heard something through the open window, I love that for you.

That was the sound of a woman finally getting what she wants, headboard slamming the wall, full volume, and not one single fuck given (pun fully intended).

CHAPTER 6

Money, Power & Other Scary Words

In my marriage the financial power dynamic was clear from the start. When I met my ex in our late 20s, I had the degree, I owned my house, and I had real money in the bank. My income and my well-paying job allowed us to buy our first home and build a comfortable life. And while that setup gave us economic stability, I now see how it might have seeded an imbalance neither of us wanted to name. Mainly, I had the money, and he had the sweat equity.

But here's the truth: Even with the financial edge, I didn't feel powerful. I sometimes felt scrutinized, moved carefully to keep the peace, and lived with a quiet worry that everything we'd built could fall apart at any moment.

I know he was proud of every raise, every stock grant, and every bonus I earned. But I never got credit for what it took to get there: the long hours, the corporate bullshit, the mental gymnastics of showing up, climbing, producing, and staying one step ahead of disaster for my kids.

I'd always lived with the fear of being on my own, and during the divorce it came true. I *was* suddenly on my own. And I *still* had to keep everything going.

Now I have my Aussie Man. Early on in our relationship my financial footing made a lot of things possible: trips, flights, experiences, logistics. But what people didn't see was me scraping together money for my boys' expenses, saving for college, and making sure they never felt the ground shake even as my world was being rocked. The power I'd built didn't come overnight. It came at a cost. It was built on worry, on grind, on fear-fueled forward motion.

It was built on a belief I'd held since I was young: that the only way to stay safe was to stay prepared. That's probably why I lied about my age to get my first job at 14. It wasn't because I needed money. (In fact, my mom provided *everything*.)

Instead, it was because life with my dad and in proximity to my parents' relationship felt so out of control that earning money became my armor. Money meant I didn't have to rely on anyone. It meant I could leave if I had to. It gave me options. When you've grown up waiting for the other shoe to drop, *that's* power.

Even now, after decades of stockpiling security, I can still feel the ghost of that scared girl bracing for impact. But she didn't break. She built.

And she made sure her boys wouldn't grow up thinking comfort came from someone else's wallet or required someone else's permission.

Real Girls Guide To Money Mantras: A cheat sheet.

When I spoke with Liz Svatek, Podcaster and Author of *Finding Your Diamonds*, about ambition and power, she dismantled the tired idea that drive automatically equals cutthroat competition. Midlife women know better—we've been through enough boardrooms, breakups, and breakdowns to see that power isn't about hoarding—it's about amplifying. Ambition here doesn't scorch the earth, it plants seeds. As Liz says: "Ambition in midlife isn't ruthless—it's collaborative, contagious, and legacy-driven."

This line anchors our discussion, which explores how midlife women are redefining power—not as domination, but as expression, freedom, and legacy. It reflects the shift from climbing ladders to building ecosystems where other women rise, too.

10 Money Mantras for Real Girls:

1. Money was never just money.

It was power. It was safety. It was control when the rest of your life felt like a wrecking ball.

2. Your paycheck isn't your worth.

You can make six figures and still feel like you're one bad day away from collapse. That's not failure, it's trauma. Name it so you can stop living in it.

3. Solo hustle built you, but it doesn't have to define you.

Being the breadwinner taught you grit. Now you get to choose rest without guilt. That's not lazy. That's earned.

4. You don't owe anyone a power struggle.

Just because you *can* do it all doesn't mean you have to prove it every day. Let your partner carry some weight. The world won't end.

5. Old scarcity mindsets die hard.

That urge to squirrel away cash and wait for the sky to fall? It's your nervous system talking. Remind it you're not that 14-year-old anymore.

(continued)

6.   It's OK to want nice shit.

The car, the trip, the splurge-y bottle of wine? If you can afford it and it brings joy, not chaos, you don't have to justify it. Joy is ROI, too.

7.   Reinvention isn't just a buzzword.

It's a slow, messy, liberating unraveling of what you thought success had to look like. And it's worth every uncomfortable second.

8.   Dependency doesn't equal weakness.

Letting someone support you doesn't erase the decades you supported everyone else. It just means you're finally safe enough to exhale.

9.   If it's not on your terms, it's not power.

Consulting part-time? Writing your truth? Sleeping the hell in? That's control. That's power. That's midlife done right.

10. You get to keep the credit.

For the nights you didn't sleep. For the jobs you never quit. For holding the line when no one else could. Even now... especially now... you get to own that story. Loudly.

Bonus: Real Girls affirmations for women who've paid the bills:

- I am the CFO of my own life.
- I don't need permission to buy peace of mind.
- I built this safety net, I can use it.
- Power isn't greedy, it's grounding.
- My money, my rules, my future.

Money, power, and the midlife mindfuck of letting go.

None of this talk is about retirement calculators or compound interest. It's about what happens when money stops being your survival strategy and starts asking you to share the steering wheel. Power, control, fear, identity, welcome to the emotional shitshow that is midlife money.

My ability to pay the bills, fund the vacations, save for college, and still manage to keep the lights on (emotionally and literally) when everything around me felt one missed paycheck away from collapse wasn't just about security.

It was power. It was survival. It was how I stayed ahead of the chaos.

Fast-forward to now: I have a partner, a shared life, and a totally different financial rhythm. My man built a company from the ground up, and while I "funded the first eight years," as he likes to say, now he's funding our next chapter.

For the first time I'm not grinding solo. And holy shit that shift is both freeing and disorienting!

I felt the tectonic plates of identity move under me. Could I still call myself independent? Was I losing credibility? Was I giving up too much of the badass who got us here in the first place?

Not really. I'm not losing myself, I'm just evolving.

These days, I'm consulting part-time. I wrote this book. And I'm reclaiming my time. Not in the "ladies who lunch" sense but in the *this is for me, by me, and fully on my term's* kind of way. (Although if anyone wants to start a Match.com-style app for finding badass women available for noon cocktails, hit me up.)

Because here's the thing: financial power in midlife hits different, it's not just about the hustle. It's about choice. Ownership. Knowing you've earned the right to *not* kill yourself to prove your worth.

Retirement? That word looks different for every woman I know. One friend's about to become a grandma. Another is starting over after her

30-year marriage blew up. And me? I'm trying to dodge grandma status for another decade while building a next chapter with my man—one that creates room for us, our kids, and all the magic they haven't seen yet.

This dialogue is for every woman who's ever equated her worth with her W-2. Every woman who's struggled to let go of the "I got this" identity even when someone's stepping up. Every woman who's unlearning the notion that needing support isn't weakness, it's shared power.

And yeah, it's still terrifying. But also? It's time.

Expert Q&A with Kathy Criscuolo Boufford: Attorney & Author of *Divorce Matters*

Kathy Boufford is a dedicated family attorney, trial advocate, and mediator with more than 30 years of experience practicing law in Connecticut. She's also the author of *Divorce Matters*, a guide that cuts through the chaos to help women navigate divorce with clarity, confidence, and a hell of a lot less regret. Here's why this matters now: The U.S. divorce rate is currently 2.4 per 1000 people, 40% of first marriages end, and women initiate nearly 70% of all divorces. "Grey divorces" aka splits after 50, are on the rise, bringing new complications around identity, money, adult children, and decades of shared life.

Her book is about sidestepping the most common landmines: emotional, legal, and financial. It offers straight-up guidance on everything from picking the right professionals and prepping your documents, to navigating mental health issues, custody, or mediation. It doesn't promise "easy," but it does promise you won't be alone, confused, or steamrolled if you read it.

Q: What should women over 50 know before they drop the D-bomb?
A: *Start early. If you're even thinking about divorce, get your ducks in*

*a row—quietly. Find your own financial advisor (not one you share),
start estimating your cost of living post-divorce, and figure out what
assets and income are on the table. Pay cash when you consult a lawyer
so it's not traceable. Emotionally, give yourself space to grieve. Most
of us have been married longer than we've been single. Your identity
is wrapped up in "we"—this is the moment you start rebuilding "me."
And know this: not everyone will handle it well. Divorce shakes up
family dynamics, especially with adult kids. Expect side-taking. Be
kind, but don't pull people into the mess. Protect your peace.*

**Q: How do we stop romanticizing marriage and start
protecting ourselves?**

A: *You can be in love and still protect your damn self. Have the hard
financial talks before you're legally tangled. Debt? Spending styles?
Career expectations? Lay it all out. And yes—prenups aren't unro-
mantic. They're smart. Also, always have your own bank account,
credit card, and cash. Even in the happiest relationships, financial
autonomy is power. No one should be stuck because they can't afford
to leave.*

Q: What's "silent divorcing" and how can we spot it?

A: *Silent divorce is a quiet drift. You're still technically married—but
emotionally, it's over. You co-exist, co-parent, share space, but the intimacy, connection, and future dreams are gone. You live parallel lives.
No yelling, no cheating, just... nothing. It's common in long marriages.
Often people wake up in their 60s, staring down retirement, and
think, 'Is this all there is?' Or the kids leave and you realize you don't
even recognize the person across the table. If that's you? You're not
crazy. You're not alone. And you don't have to stay stuck.*

**Q: How can midlife women reclaim power instead of
getting steamrolled?**

A: *Learn everything. Knowledge is power. Read, talk to professionals,
get advice from people who've been through it. The unknown is scary
but once you know your rights and your options, it gets a whole lot*

less terrifying. And remember: Just because you're starting over at 40, 50 or 60 doesn't mean you're late. You're just on a different timeline. Like I always say, "You don't need a brand-new start, you just need a brand-new ending."

Even when money can't buy fun, it sure as hell buys freedom.

Lying to get my first job at 14 wasn't about ambition or some cute coming-of-age hustle, it was about control, plain and simple. I wasn't hustling for fun or saving up for concert tickets. None of my friends had jobs. My parents weren't pushing me to work.

But life at home had started to feel shaky, and something in me knew I needed a lifeline. So, I strolled into a strip-mall salon, lied about my age, and snagged a $4.50-an-hour cashier gig. Why? Because even then I knew if the ground was going to shake, I wanted to be the one holding the railing. When I got that first paycheck, reality hit like a brick. After taxes, it was essentially just lint and a few sad pennies.

But you know what? It was *mine*.

I took it straight to Macy's and bought a Liz Claiborne wallet to put my basically nonexistent funds into. That purchase wasn't about fashion. It was about claiming my own identity, even if it was stitched into faux leather and cost more than I probably made in two shifts.

Fast forward to my first "real" job post-college: $24K a year, and I thought I was rich. I scraped together what was left of my college account (thanks, Dad), put a down payment on a tiny house, and thought I'd built a fortress against the chaos I grew up around.

Spoiler: A mortgage doesn't protect you from life imploding, but it sure gives you a false sense of security.

I lived on PB&J so religiously that when my dad visited and opened my dishwasher, he asked why there were only knives inside. My answer? That's all I needed for my poor-girl diet plan. No plates. No spoons. Just survival, baby.

And that was the beginning of me learning that money wasn't just about stuff: It was about safety, about not needing anyone, about being three steps ahead of the next disaster.

5 Real Girls Experts on Money, Power, and Other Scary Words

Money is never just money. It's power, control, shame, freedom, identity. And in midlife it all comes roaring to the surface. Whether you've been the breadwinner for decades or just started learning the difference between a Roth IRA and GTFO, this chapter is for the women grappling with what it means to hold (or hand over) the financial reins.

Here are five big, bold truths from the experts and thinkers helping us redefine what wealth, ambition and financial power look like—Spanx off, eyes open, and accounts finally balanced.

1. Your value is not your paycheck.

"Ambition changes shape. And women's power grows when they stop tying self-worth to what they earn."

—TARA MOHR, Author of *Playing Big*

Whether you opted out, scaled down, or un-retired to launch something brand new, your worth isn't hiding in a direct deposit. Midlife ambition? It's quieter, but sharper. It's about legacy, not ladders. Purpose, not promotion.

2. Breadwinning isn't masculine, it's mastery.

"There is nothing unfeminine about making your own money. What's

radical is doing it your way, unapologetically."

—FARNOOSH TORABI, Author of *When She Makes More*

More women in midlife are primary earners or sole providers, by choice, by chance, or by sheer grit. That can rock relationship dynamics, especially if a partner's ego hasn't caught up. But Farnoosh's advice? Don't shrink. Lead the financial conversation with confidence and clarity.

3. Don't just save. Own.

"We've spent decades saving for security. Now we need to invest in sovereignty." —JACQUETTE TIMMONS, Financial Behaviorist

Security is important, but so is agency. It's time to move beyond passive saving and into active ownership: of assets, decisions, and dreams. Jacquette challenges women to make money decisions from a place of power, not fear.

4. Financial shame is inherited but doesn't have to be yours.

"We inherit financial narratives from our families, but we don't have to live them." —AMANDA CLAYMAN, Financial Therapist

Your money story might come with guilt, fear, or a sense that it's never enough. That's not yours to carry. Amanda helps women unpack that baggage and replace it with clarity, control, and a little swagger. Money management isn't just spreadsheets, it's self-respect.

5. Money is a mirror. And midlife is a good time to look.

"Your relationship with money is your relationship with yourself, in numbers." —LYNNE TWIST, Author of *The Soul of Money*

(continued)

Midlife doesn't lie. Neither does your budget. But Lynne reminds us: the goal isn't just more, it's meaning. What you spend, save, and give should reflect your values. Financial health isn't about hoarding, it's about flow, generosity, and joy.

Why old money habits die hard (and how to let them die anyway).

Oh, I'm unlearning a *lot* about money and power. Let's just say it's not a gentle process.

I had an unhealthy relationship with money for decades. Not in the flashy, reckless way, either. It was more like I had a white-knuckle grip on money because I believed it was the only thing keeping me safe. Money meant control. Control meant security. Security meant survival. I worked my ass off starting as a teenager and never stopped.

Hustle was (maybe still is) my love language. Quitting wasn't an option. It felt like failure.

Which is probably why I stayed too long in jobs that drained me, worked under toxic bosses, and tolerated being undervalued by women who should've known better. (Shoutout to my then 12-year-old son for calling it "friendly fire" when I couldn't see it myself.)

Somewhere deep down I think I believed I had to take the hits and eat the shit, that maybe I didn't deserve better. That if I didn't earn love, worth, or peace through hard work, I wasn't worthy of having it.

But now? I'm rewriting that story.

I'm learning that power doesn't have to come from a paycheck. Stability doesn't only live in a savings account. And security isn't tied to how many hours I grind. I'm done hoarding fear like it's a coupon code for survival. I've torched the scarcity mindset and I'm grabbing joy, power, and peace with both hands.

None of it's tied to a paycheck.

Case in point: I recently bought myself a car—a fancy one. It happened on a whim while spending time with my man, who was in town that day. I wrote a big-ass check. Drove it home. Waited for the wave of guilt or panic or buyer's remorse to roll in the next morning when I walked into the garage.

Turns out, it didn't.

In my past, I long held the belief that I had to earn love, and I had a fear of scarcity with money. For me, money needed to take care of my survival. But buying that car felt the opposite—I earned my money, I earned my pride and I bought a car I felt like I fucking deserved. I didn't care what anyone else thought. Did I need a fancy car? Nope. I wanted it.

Final Takeaway

Whether you're rebuilding after divorce, launching a second-act business or figuring out what "enough" looks like after years of over functioning, the real flex isn't just earning. It's owning. And redefining power not as something you fight for, but something you already have.

Midlife money isn't scary. It's sacred.

And we're done being quiet about it.

CHAPTER 7

Getting Uncomfortable on Purpose

Midlife can be liberating, and for some women it's an opportunity to shed the past and take a massive leap of faith. My boldest change came back in 2019 when I walked away from a wildly successful job where I had the title, the track record, and the financial wins. On paper it was perfect.

But in my gut? I wanted more. Specifically, I wanted to be part of a company going public. It was a dream I'd shelved for years.

So, I took the risk. Left safety. Bet on myself.

I took a new job at an enterprise preparing to go public.

Six months before the IPO, our company lost its marketing leader, the person I reported directly to. In their absence, there was no one to steer the ship from a marketing perspective. When a company is on the fast track to being listed on a stock exchange, let's just say the marketing department becomes *very* important, and *very* scrutinized.

For me, stepping up meant no fancy title change. No raise.

Just the void, and me, standing there with the instincts, the experience, and the fire to fill it. So, I led. I made the calls. Built the workstreams. Took the hits. Scheduled weekly "spiral sessions" with a trusted teammate just to survive the chaos.

And I did more than survive. I crushed it. On IPO day, I handed the reins over to the new Chief Marketing Officer with a deep, soul-level pride. Not performative pride, the real kind. The kind that says: *I did a brilliant fucking job.*

All those years of wondering if I needed someone to *choose* me. I finally asked the better question: *Why not me?*

That's the question I come back to every time I'm afraid. Every time the self-doubt creeps in. Because the truth is, I didn't just step up, I *had* it in me all along. I just finally stopped asking for permission to show it.

This next life chapter? It's still scary. I'm rebuilding on my terms. Writing this book. Advising leaders. Navigating shared finances after years of doing it alone. Feeling empowered *and* uncertain, sometimes in the same breath.

But I'm done pretending those contradictions mean I'm lost.

They mean I'm growing.

So, to every woman staring down a leap later in life, whether it's a career change, a new dream, a fresh start, or all three, hear me:

You don't need a map. You need a moment.

Your moment to say: Why not me?

And then go do the thing.

Expert Q&A with Bronwyn Saglimbeni:
Entrepreneur & Founder of Bronwyn
Communications

When I first met Bronwyn Saglimbeni back in the early 2000s, she was already a PR force of nature. Then she did what most of us spend our lives avoiding—she got uncomfortable. She walked away from a safe, successful career and built BRONWYN Communications from the ground up, coaching business and world leaders to shine in their biggest front-facing moments—her clients have appeared on everything from *American Idol* to *Real Time with Bill Maher* to *The Oprah Winfrey Show* and TEDx stages around the world.

Bronwyn's story isn't just about communication, it's about grit, confidence, and what happens when you lean all the way into discomfort and come out the other side a complete and total badass.

Q: What did you have to unlearn about "success" to pivot this hard in midlife?

A: *The pivot came from collapse—of will, interest, and my career identity. Fifteen years in, on vacation in Sicily, I remember collapsing on the bed thinking: 'I built a career that's actively trying to kill me.' What if I cut out the parts making me sick and sad—what's left? Storytelling. Connecting with audiences. But the next voice kicked in: 'You can't make money doing that—no healthcare, no safety net.' Men burn the boats. Women don't. Year one? Ten percent of my old income—but I knew I'd grow the pie away from PR and into a super-niche consulting practice where I could make great money and build long-term relationships, not churn-and-burn projects. It was also the TED era—Steve Jobs, big ideas, cultural magic. I targeted TED Talk clients, charged almost nothing at first, then Stanford came aboard. The vibe was irresistible. It wasn't about packaging myself—it was about the work. I wanted people to dream bigger on stage, and I showed them what was possible.*

Q: How did you get past the fear of being seen—older, bolder, and in a totally new arena?

A: *It wasn't stage fright. It was the voice: 'Who does she think she is?' My relationship to performance is rooted in service. I want to be a blessing in someone's life. Big swings mean risk. Sometimes it's humiliating. But like Amy Poehler says, "Power is not caring if you look stupid." I had to sign that contract: If you say yes to a big, bold life, you're agreeing to awkwardness, to wipeouts, to imperfection. That's the only way to live big.*

Q: What does ambition look like now—and how has your definition of power shifted since your time in PR?

A: *I'm still wrestling with this. I used to think power was status: the car, the title, the house, the room that goes silent when you walk in. Now? Real power is sovereignty. The ability to leave rooms, jobs, relationships that ask me to shrink or betray myself. High-quality yeses and noes—and owning the consequences. On the other side of sovereignty is peace. That's the power play now.*

Q: What role has discomfort played in your biggest leaps— and how do you know when it's time to leap again?

A: *Discomfort is the number one catalyst in my life. The pain of staying put finally outweighs the fear of change. I can sit in denial too long, endure too much. But every joyful leap came from listening to what felt expansive, never from gritting it out. The hardest part? The in-between—knowing X isn't working but Y hasn't revealed itself yet. That's the endurance test: waiting for clarity while sitting in the mess.*

Q: What message are you most proud to put into the world now that it's your voice behind the mic?

A: *That the time is now. We wait for permission, for credibility, for some mythical moment of "arrival." It doesn't exist. We're all messy, we all have imposter syndrome, we're all winging it. The sooner we get comfortable with that, the sooner we speak up and claim our lives. No more waiting.*

How to rewrite those old, nagging, untrue stories.

In my experience, the most damaging stories in life are usually the oldest ones, the mythologized ones from the deepest, darkest parts of our memory. The ones that got whispered to us before we even had the words to push back. The ones we absorbed from bosses who overlooked us, cultures that devalued us, and even our own inner monologue.

Now, I'm calling bullshit on the story that we're too old to change. Too late to matter. Too tired to lead. Approaching this age hasn't felt like a gentle birthday, it's felt like a blinking neon sign screaming: *Time's flying, babe. Bust a move.*

And I am. Because here's what I've learned: no one is coming to grant you permission. You either take the leap or you stay stuck in some-one else's idea of who you're supposed to be. After my "un-retirement," something busted wide open. I realized I'd been carrying around stories that didn't belong to me:

- That I wasn't strategic enough.
- That I was just "good help."
- That I should be grateful for flexibility instead of aiming for power.
- That choosing motherhood meant I'd forfeited ambition.

Bull. Fucking. Shit.

Those stories didn't just hold me back, they *shrunk* me. I played smaller than I was. I waited to be asked in instead of walking through the door I built myself. But when I transitioned and stepped into advisory roles with CMOs and CEOs, I saw the truth: I didn't need to audition. I'd already earned my place. The strategies I delivered? Nailed it. The instincts? Rock solid. The wisdom? Bought and paid for with 30 years of wins, scars, and pure hustle. Now, I do the work because I *want* to. Not because I need to prove anything.

And if you're reading this thinking it's too late to start over, to shift gears, to bet on yourself, I want you to hear this:

You're not late, you're loaded.
With firepower.
With pattern recognition.
With gut instinct.
With resilience 25-year-olds haven't even dreamed of yet.

So, rewrite the story. Make the pivot. Take the risk.

The Real Girl in you is ready.

She's not waiting anymore.

Real Girls Reality Check(list):
Rewrite the rules of your midlife power move.

Here's your no-BS guide to midlife career pivots, purpose shifts and stepping into the power you've *always* had. Yes, it will be uncomfortable. And yes, you *can* do this.

1. Burn the old script.

Stop waiting for permission. You are not an intern. You don't need a mentor to validate your next move. You need a match to spark and a clear view of what's no longer serving you.

2. Fact-check the story you've been telling yourself.

"I'm not strategic."
"I'm not visible."
"I'm just execution."

Sound familiar? Real Girls challenge the lies they've outgrown.

3. Name what you actually want.

Not what you *should* want. Not what fits on a resume. What do *you* want to build, solve, create, or walk away from? Write it down. Say it out loud.

4. Stop discounting survival as strategy.

The years you spent holding everything together weren't "lost." They made you powerful. Resourceful. Dangerous in the best way.

5. Use every ounce of your firepower.

Your experience is your leverage. Your intuition is your data. Your scars are strategy maps. Act accordingly.

6. Redefine risk.

Is it risky to pivot now? Or is it riskier to stay small? Real Girls take bets on themselves, even when (and maybe especially when) the odds aren't guaranteed.

7. Find work that matches your energy, not just your skillset.

Screw "qualified." Find what lights you up, pisses you off, or makes you pound the table. Follow *that*.

8. Kill the comparison game.

She got the TED Talk. She wrote the book. She launched the brand. Cool. You've got your own lane. Drive it like you stole it.

9. Surround yourself with bold women who say: 'Do it.'

You don't need cheerleaders. You need co-conspirators. Women who see your worth and don't flinch when you go big.

10. Make noise, take up space and don't shrink to fit.

You're not a vibe. You're a force. Walk into every room like your future depends on it. Because it does.

How (and why) I've modeled resilience through discomfort with my family.

My kids have heard a lot of my go-to mantras (aka MOMtras) over the years: *Make good choices. When people show you who they are, believe them. And if you're going to take a risk, bet on yourself.*

But the truth is, the most powerful lessons I've taught them didn't come from lectures. They came from watching me *live* that shit. They saw it when I walked away from that secure, high-paying job in 2019 to take a leap on a scrappy, pre-IPO company because I believed in my gut and bet on myself.

They saw it when their dad and I divorced, not because it was easy but because I knew I deserved more—hell, we both did. I deserved someone who *chose me*. Who fought for me. Who lit up because of our partnership. And I wasn't going to settle for less just to keep that "perfect" picture intact.

They've seen me fall apart. Cry from exhaustion. Crack under the pressure of trying to hold *everything*—motherhood, work, finances, survival, sanity—together. But what I hope they've really seen is this: It's OK to bend. It's even OK to feel like you might break.

But then? You *rise*. You act. You move.

You don't freeze. You don't wallow. You don't wait for someone to rescue you. You don't assume the role of victim. Resilience isn't about being unshakeable. It's about getting back up when life tries to take you out and saying: *Not today.*

I tell my kids all the time: Doing nothing is a choice. But so is doing something.

And in my house? We *do something*.

Midlife Pivots, 'Why Not Me?' Moments, and Crashing Your Old Identity on Purpose

Midlife doesn't tap gently, it crashes in with a WTF and a side of holy hell. The job titles don't mean what they used to. The hustle starts to feel like punishment. And the life you built so carefully starts itching like a wool sweater in August. These are the stories of ladies who stopped waiting for clarity, comfort, or permission, and started tearing down the parts of their lives that no longer fit. Some walked away from careers. Some melted down behind closed doors. Some built something new in secret while holding it all together in public. None of it was easy. All of it was brave.

Nikki: VP, Mom, Wife, and still herself.

Nikki is a high-powered VP in her 40s, raising little kids, commuting daily, juggling a demanding career and a family calendar that looks like air traffic control. On paper, it's all working.

In reality? The pressure to be exceptional in every role—mom, leader, wife, daughter—was suffocating. "I was trying so hard to be the best at everything that I couldn't breathe. There were days I'd crush a board meeting and then cry in the carpool line because I forgot it was pajama day," Nikki says.

She's still in it. Still doing the dance. But something shifted. She started asking what *she* needed, not just what her team, her kids, or her partner needed. She's learning to drop the stick she's been beating herself with. Letting "good enough" be a radical act of self-preservation. "It's not about balance, that's a lie," she says. "It's about being honest about what matters and finally being okay with disappointing people if it means not disappearing."

(continued)

Missy: The pivot you can't unsee.

At 51, Missy walked away from a 27-year career working on Hollywood film and TV stages. She had a mortgage, two kids in college, and no plan, just a deep gut-truth that she couldn't grind through one more shoot day pretending she loved it. "Something cracked open in me," she says, "This quiet voice whispering, *Why not you? Why not now?*"

She leaned all the way in. Trained as an energy healer. Built a business from scratch. Posted her first video with shaky, nervous hands and started charging for her worth. Within three years, she was earning more than she did working in her old union job, all while helping women worldwide reclaim their power. "Resilience isn't about bouncing back, it's about becoming more *you* with every risk you take," says Missy.

Sarah: The value crisis.

Sarah's identity crash came not from what she started, but what she stopped. She left her job in her late 30s and suddenly didn't know who she was. "No paycheck. No title. No power. Just me, wondering if I still had value without a promotion or a 401(k)," she says. Leaning on her husband financially for the first time felt like pulling her own teeth. But she realized the real issue wasn't the money, it was the worth. Learning to see herself as valuable without earning it was the most rebellious thing she'd ever done.

Florence: When the Zooms stack high.

Florence didn't burn it all down. She just started telling the truth. "It was a slow death by calendar invite," she says. The endless meetings. The performative productivity. The hunger to be seen and the fear of stopping. Until one day, she did stop. And in the stillness, she remembered who she was before every hour of her day got filled. "I had to walk away from the external validation machine," says Florence. "My value isn't in how many boxes I tick, it's in how I feel when I wake up."

The Takeaway

These women didn't pivot because it was cute or trendy. They did it because staying the same was killing them slowly. Because something inside them whispered: *Why not me?* These stories are for every woman sitting in her car, in her office, or on her bathroom floor wondering if it's too late.

It's not. You're right on time.

What the experts taught me about uncomfortable transformations.

The most powerful insight I've taken from studying change experts is this—transformation doesn't come from clarity, it comes from motion. The experts who truly move people don't hand them a blueprint. They help them get unstuck. They remind us that waiting for the "right time" or the "perfect plan" is just fear in a fancy outfit.

For women in midlife, that hits hard. We've been conditioned to believe that our big changes are behind us. That reinvention is for the young.

But the truth? *We're just getting started*. The job, the marriage, the body, the belief system—we can change all of it. And we don't need permission.

So, here's the Real Girls call to action: Don't wait to feel ready. Move anyway. Say yes to the thing that scares you. Start the conversation. Take the class. Send the pitch. Book the solo trip. Cut your hair. Reinvention isn't a luxury. It's our *birthright*.

Expert Q&A with Lisa Martin: Tech Broadcaster, Analyst and Former Host of *theCube*

Lisa Martin isn't just translating tech—she's redefining what power, presence, and reinvention look like after 50. With over two decades in enterprise media and more than 650 on-camera interviews with global execs (yes, even Michael Dell), Lisa brings sharp insight and unmatched polish to every conversation. Before becoming one of Silicon Valley's go-to tech broadcasters, Lisa was a payload scientist at NASA. (Pause to let that brilliance sink in.) Today, she's the voice behind *CMOs: Unscripted*, appears regularly on Techstrong TV and Bloomberg, and leads Lisa Martin Media, her boutique agency helping enterprise brands shape strategy and story.

We sat down with Lisa to talk on-camera confidence, career pivots, public voice in midlife, and why reinvention is just another kind of rocket science.

Q: You spent years building a badass reputation in tech marketing—what was the moment (or meltdown) that made you say, "Screw it, I'm doing something completely different?"

A: *Actually, the first moment was after I had been hit by a car while walking in a crosswalk in my neighborhood, which broke my left arm in half. Then a few months later I felt a lump in my right breast, and it terrified me. I was so fortunate that it was just a cyst, but it was the catalyst I needed to launch my own marketing agency in the tech industry. The second moment was totally fear-based, when I ended up in a shock divorce situation. I made the decision then that I would try my hardest to grow my company so I could continue doing what I love professionally. It was hard, but I did it, I am doing it!*

Q: Midlife isn't exactly when society tells us to start over, especially not on camera. What old story did you have to burn down to make space for this new version of you?

A: *That I would be invalidated by no longer being someone's wife. I was able to rebuild my life from the ground up, literally. I fought hard, did lots of therapy and introspection to learn what my role in the marriage breakdown was. And I became publicly vulnerable. The latter was eye-opening for me. I started to see that the more honest (and vulnerable) I was, people respected me and opened up. It was a refreshing realization.*

Q: Broadcast isn't for the faint of heart, especially when you're not 27 and TikTok-famous. What's one myth about visibility, age, or "starting over" you've personally blown to bits?

A: *That age is your rate limiter. It can be, but it doesn't have to be! Many people believe that their age is a barrier to starting something new or gaining visibility in their industry. But, let me tell you, from my high school days on, I always thought I missed my calling to be a news anchor. Well, thanks to my network and my work ethic, I was able to successfully break into broadcasting at the age of 41. I've seen many others successfully transition to new careers, build their professional brand, and achieve their goals at various stages of their lives. It can absolutely be done!*

Q: Let's talk balls (metaphorical, of course): Where did you find the courage to bet on yourself, and what advice do you give other women whose dreams are still whispering at them from the back seat?

A: *Well, during and after my divorce I really had no other choice but to bet on myself... What if it's always going to be just me (and my dogs)? I had to prepare for that and face my fears of being alone. It sucks, but it's my current reality. I'm working hard to change that, but I have to continue to bet on myself. At the end of the day, I can only count on myself.*

Q: What's one thing this chapter of your career has given you that no corporate climb ever did and what would your 30-year-old self never believe about where you are now?
A: *Confidence. I would tell my 30-year-old self to believe in herself. I made a major career pivot in my early 30s, from being a scientist with NASA to working in tech (sales, then marketing the last 20 years), so why couldn't I take a big leap again? With a little confidence and a good reputation and network, that's how I got into tech broadcasting and now I'm on iHeartRadio twice weekly as a tech expert and featured on TV programs like Schwab Network. Anything is possible!*

5 Real Girls Questions I'd ask a Hollywood legend about her own bold moves at midlife: An intentionally abstract interview.

Real Talk: Who is the one woman I'd put front and center in the "Real Girls Hall of Courageous Reinvention?"

Jamie Lee Curtis. That's right, the legendary 1980s scream queen.

Why? First off, I'm a huge fan of the *Halloween* movie franchise. In fact, I made my boys watch all 13 installments one October a few years back. Secondly, her stint on another favorite show of mine, *The Real Housewives of Beverly Hills*, was a truly magical moment on my TV screen. Lastly, and most importantly, she's loud (in the best way possible). She's liberated. She's aging and not asking for permission or giving a damn about anyone's approval. She's ditched the Hollywood smoke and mirrors for something way more radical: truth and self-possession.

She's been open about sobriety (preach), about body image (I direct you back to Chapter 2), about getting old (it happens to us all), about beauty without the bullshit (well, this entire book in a way). She shows up on red carpets in her 60s with gray hair and a spine of steel and somehow makes *real* look iconic.

So, if I had five minutes and five questions with Jamie Lee, I'd ask her these questions:

1. What did you have to unlearn to finally feel free in your skin?
2. How do you protect your peace in a world that profits off women feeling 'not enough?'
3. What's one beauty standard you wish we could burn to the ground for good?
4. Have you ever been underestimated in your second (or third) act? If so, how did you respond?
5. What would you say to the woman in her 50s who feels invisible, exhausted, and afraid it's 'too late?'

And what do I *hope* she'd say?

> Answer 1: *Midlife isn't the afterthought. It's the main event.*
> Answer 2: *Being real beats being perfect.*
> Answer 3: *Courage doesn't always roar, sometimes it's just showing up exactly as you are.*
> Answer 4: *As for women over 50? We're just getting dangerous.*
> Answer 5: *The lines and the silver? They're proof we've lived, and they look good on us.*

How this whole book writing journey reflects my embrace of the super uncomfortable.

Picture this: We're on the couch, coffee in hand. Mine has too much cream and sugar, but who cares? You've just asked me a profound question: "When did you last leap? And what did it teach you?"

Here's the truth: I've been carrying this book idea since I was 35. Back then it showed up as scribbled notes in the margins of work decks, voice memos I'd whisper into during preschool pickups, and late-night journal entries I never let see the light of day. The voice inside me was loud, but life got messier.

So, I shelved it. Buried it under parenting, marriage, career ladders, divorce, new love, old grief, teen meltdowns, kid logistics, and the million ways women over function their way through life. But the story never left. It just sat patiently, maybe even a little pissed, waiting for me to be ready. And then in my mid-50s, retired for a month, and something split open. It wasn't some cute movie montage where everything clicks into place. It felt more like standing barefoot on broken glass—painful and way too real. I wasn't fearless. I was raw. Vulnerable. Unsteady. Wide open.

But somewhere inside all that discomfort, I caught a glimpse of the woman I always was but spent too many years dimming down to make space for everyone else. So, I started writing. Again. For real this time.

This book, REAL GIRLS GUIDE TO MIDLIFE? It wasn't just a project. It was a reckoning. It was me unearthing the version of myself I'd tucked away under all the titles, to-do lists, and polite smiles. It was me, finally telling the truth, even when it was messy, especially when it was messy.

And every day I sat down to write, I remembered this: I am scared shitless. But I'm doing it anyway. Because the real flex at this age isn't perfection. It's choosing *yourself*—loudly, unapologetically, and without waiting for someone else to say, "You're allowed."

If you're sitting there thinking, *I missed my moment*, let me be the first one to call bullshit. You didn't miss the boat, you *are* the boat. The waves. The whole beautiful ocean. Now go start your thing. Pick up the pen, open the laptop, enroll in the class, walk into the room, speak the idea out loud.

I did it, messy, scared and late by every metric.

But also, right on time. And so are you.

CHAPTER 8

Speaking Up Because You Can

If I'm being 100% to-the-core level honest, I stayed silent for *way too fucking long*. I swallowed my feelings, bit my tongue, played peacemaker like it was a full-time job. I contorted myself into the "good girl," the "don't-rock-the-boat" girl, the "please-don't-hate-me" version that was easy to digest and impossible to hear.

And yeah, maybe it started as self-protection. But eventually it became self-erasure.

There was a stretch in my teens when silence wasn't just a habit, it was survival.

My mom, my brother, and I were stuck in a mess with my dad. "Divorce" doesn't even begin to cover it—it was lies stacked on secrets stacked on emotional mind-fuckery that I didn't have the tools to understand back then. One weekend when I was about 13, what should've been a normal post-divorce visit suddenly shifted. My dad changed our plans out of nowhere and took us out of town for reasons that, in hindsight, feel more like a cover-up than anything real.

When we got back, we walked into a room full of family and friends, and someone turned to me with narrowed eyes and asked, "So what did you do this time?" Like I was the problem. Like the grown man struggling to take responsibility had nothing to do with it. Like the weight of it all somehow belonged to me.

And that wasn't the first time. In fifth grade, I remember lying on the couch with a high fever, barely conscious. My dad walked in, took one look, and scolded me—for being sick. Told me I was stressing everyone out. Now, as an adult, I can extend him some grace for being a young dad overwhelmed and carrying his own shit and stress. But in that moment, all I felt was the sting of believing that my very existence was too much.

Let that land: It felt like my existence was an inconvenience.

Those moments? They're carved deep into me. And I carried those emotional scars with me right into adulthood. At work, in my marriage, even in the early days with my now-partner. I kept quiet. Bit my lip until it bled. Told myself: *Suck it up, buttercup.*

I wore that line like armor. It was my mantra. Peace at all costs. Quiet at all costs. *Even if it meant losing myself in the process.* I second-guessed every feeling I had. Sat with them like uninvited guests. Ran them through an internal TSA checkpoint: *Are you valid? Will someone think you're too much? What will happen if you actually say this out loud?*

Tip: Nothing good ever comes from trying to play small in a life you built.

I kept thinking silence would keep the peace. That people would *get it* without me having to say it. That maybe, somehow, they'd feel the weight of what I *wasn't* saying. They didn't.

And even if they had, it wouldn't have mattered. Because that silence? It wasn't for them. It was supposed to be for me. But I gave away my voice pretending it was something noble. I choked down truth to keep other people comfortable. I minimized myself to protect their egos. Never again.

Because now, when I speak, it's not to prove anything. It's not to get permission. It's not to ask for space. It's to take it. And when I go quiet now? It's not because I'm scared, ashamed, or backing down.

It's because I *own* the moment, and I don't owe anyone an explanation.

My family history? Where do I start?

Family dynamics are complicated, it's a simple, yet common refrain. Mine, as I've come to learn through the years, might have been a little more complicated than normal. Maybe *a lot* more.

I grew up in a very tight-knit family. My mom (the only girl among four siblings) married at a young age, gave birth to me less than a year later, and went back to work just six weeks after that.

From that moment on my maternal grandparents became a constant presence in my life—and my brother's too when he came along. They watched us before and after school until we could drive, ferried us to activities, helped with homework, got us ready for big events, made Halloween costumes, chaperoned field trips, you name it. We ate countless dinners at their table, along with even more lunches and early morning breakfasts, and spent more nights under their roof than I could ever begin to count.

Their house was our second home (and in some ways felt like our primary one) and it was rarely ever just them. Aunts, uncles, cousins, great grandmas (I had two who lived there until my early teen years), even my dad's parents (and his sisters) who lived nearby, all circled around us. Even after the separation of my parents, my dad's family remained close to us all, thankfully.

The street where we all lived was practically a family compound; my grandma's cousin lived next door and an aunt across the street, and even the neighbors who weren't our blood relatives were all connected somehow.

It was like something out of a Martin Scorsese film, without all the violence and Mafia stuff.

My great-grandmother on my mom's side lived with my grandparents until I was about 13 (when she passed away). First, in the small apartment above their garage (which my grandpa had built for her when they purchased their house), and later in the main house after my mom and her brothers grew up and moved out. When my parents first married that apartment was their home, too, and where they lived when I was born. Over the years, many of my cousins (and me) rotated through that same space on our way from childhood to independence.

So many of my best memories live in that house (my uncle owns it now) and on that street—wrapped in the noise, the love, the chaos of our big Italian life—just around the corner from my childhood best friend, the daughter of my mom's best friend, who when they were young, lived across the street.

The relationship between my parents was very complicated. They were young—too young, maybe—and I think a lot of what my brother and I experienced was the result of wrong people, wrong time. Not all marriages were meant to last forever.

Still, I watched my mom navigate those hard years with class, grit and grace, building a life for herself and for us on her own terms (of course with the help of our family when we needed it). She modeled what it looked like to work hard, stand on your own two feet, be the steady rock your kids could count on, and to never wait around for someone else to make things happen. All while staying "braced," ready for the other shoe to drop.

Both sets of my grandparents had long marriages, and my grandfathers were the strong, quiet, loveable, reliable men who were always there and never left. But, it was my grandmothers who carried this quiet, no-nonsense strength I admired and wanted to emulate. They were the backbone, even at times when it seemed like the men unfortunately got more of the spotlight or the accolades.

Guilt & Shame:
Midlife moments with Charlie Bauman, LMFT

Midlife is full of "WTF" moments, but one of the biggest questions is this: "Why do I feel guilty for wanting something for myself?"

Here's why: Guilt is situational. It says: "*I messed up.*"

Shame is systemic. It says: "*I am messed up.*"

"We were taught to be nice, needed, and liked. Not bold, bound-aried or free," says Charlie. And for women, that shame is often the byproduct of generational socialization. From day one, most girls are trained to be accommodating, self-sacrificing, and lik-able. Which means that when you finally say "no," stop being the emotional concierge for your whole family, or simply *want more*, the first thing you feel isn't freedom, it's guilt.

But that's not your soul talking. That's your social conditioning. Charlie reminds us: "Not living up to these unspoken rules is a major source of shame. But the second you notice that guilt is just an echo of old training? You start to write new rules."

And those new rules? They sound a lot like: *I get to say no. My needs are valid.*

Being powerful isn't selfish. It's overdue.

Self-doubt vs. earned wisdom: Real Girls know the difference.

Real Talk: Self-doubt is loud, chaotic, a full-blown swirl. It's fear dressed up as humility, whispering that you're "grateful to be at the table," when deep down you know you built the fricken table. It spirals fast:

"Who do you think you are?"

"You're too late."

"Someone smarter already said this."

"Maybe you're not ready."

Self-doubt wants to keep you safe.
But what it *really* does is keep you small.
And quiet.
And stuck.

For a long time, I mistook that voice for caution. For practicality. For being wise. But let me tell you what real wisdom sounds like:

Wisdom is quieter, but she cuts deeper.
She doesn't spiral.
She lands.
Right in your gut.

She says:
"You've done this before."
"This isn't your lane."
"You're tired for a reason. Pause."
"Save your breath. Use it where it matters."

Wisdom doesn't need proof.
She doesn't second-guess.
She *knows*.

Now, I've learned to ask myself one thing when I hesitate: Am I shrinking out of fear or standing still out of strength? If it's fear? I act anyway. If it's wisdom? I *listen*. That's the difference.

Self-doubt says: Don't try.

Wisdom says: Try smarter.

Self-doubt says: You're too much.

Wisdom says: Use your voice *where it counts*.

The shift is this:
I don't speak to prove I belong anymore.
I speak because *I know* I do. And sometimes? I stay quiet *not* because I'm afraid, but because I *choose* to be quiet. That silence isn't weakness. It's power. It's mine. So, here's what I want you to know: You don't need a mic to make noise. But if you've earned the mic? Take it.

Say the thing.
Call out the lie.
Ask for the raise.
Leave the room.

Take the risk. Write the book.

Because now? You're not doing it to prove you can. You're doing it because you *should*.

Real Girls "Speak Up" Reality Check(list)

If you experience any of these 10 signs, recognize that it's time to use your voice. Because you've earned it. Here's some times to speak up:

1. You feel the burn.

If you're clenching your jaw, holding your breath or rage-folding laundry while someone steamrolls, yeah, it's time to speak up.

(continued)

2. You're rehearsing comebacks in the shower.

If you're scripting a response days later, that moment *still* deserves your voice. Say it. Write it. Post it. Free yourself.

3. You've seen this movie before.

If the same patterns keep repeating, whether at work, in love, or in your own head, it's time to interrupt the story.

4. You're making yourself small.

Stop. Shrinking is not service. Your bigness is not a burden.

5. You're defaulting to silence instead of choice.

Not saying something should be a decision, not a fear reflex.

6. You're the only woman in the room, and you *know* better.

Say it anyway. Especially then.

7. You're explaining away your discomfort.

If you're narrating your way out of anger, frustration, or intuition, it's not doubt. It's wisdom, trust it.

8. You've survived bigger shit.

Reminder: You've raised humans, navigated heartbreak, made magic out of chaos. You can handle one hard conversation.

9. You see women around you feeling stifled.

The truth you've lived through could unlock someone else's freedom. Say it out loud.

10. You're ready for more.

Not just more peace or power, but more *you*. Unfiltered, unapologetic, unstoppable.

When *shouldn't* you speak up?
The answer might surprise you.

Here's a powerful communication insight forged from lived experience, professional grit, and a little bit of *Real Housewives* realness: The most radical act of communication is knowing when *not* to argue for your worth.

I learned this in layers. Ben Kiker, my former boss and Executive Coach, gave me one of the most transformative pieces of life advice, one I still come back to even years later: "*Let go or be dragged.*" He used to remind me to "*Observe, don't attach.*" Translation? Not every opinion is sacred. Not every critic, or criticism, deserves a rebuttal. Just because someone says it, doesn't mean you have to carry it.

And then came a moment I didn't expect from an episode of *The Real Housewives of Beverly Hills*, no less. Bozoma Saint John—yes, *that* Bozoma, former CMO of Apple Music, Netflix, Endevor, and Pepsi—told a story during one of her early episodes that hit me square in the gut.

She shared that during her time as a CMO, after years of grinding in high-visibility, high-impact roles, her boss once told her she "*didn't have enough wins on the books.*"

Let that sink in. Not enough wins. Despite transforming brands, leading iconic launches, and showing up as one of the few Black women in those executive rooms, someone still questioned whether she was "enough."

So, what did she do? She *walked*. Not because she wasn't winning, but because she wasn't going to waste another ounce of energy convincing anyone that she already had done the damn thing.

She's also talked about how even during her rise at Pepsi she felt her success was often attributed to others. That kind of erasure hits differently, especially for women who've spent decades building credibility only to have it diluted by proximity or politics. Bozoma wasn't just chasing the next title, she was fighting to be *seen* for her *own* impact.

That's the insight: At some point you stop arguing for your seat at the table and start asking, "Is this even a table I want to sit down at?"

When women in midlife are told to quiet down, stay grateful, or play small, I think of what Bozoma did—and I think of Ben's mantra. Let go of the old story. Observe who's trying to write your ending. Don't attach your worth to someone else's scoreboard. Maybe you're consulting, pivoting, re-entering, or rewriting, but it's not about how many wins someone else sees. It's about how many battles you've already survived, how much brilliance you've stopped downplaying, and how deeply you *know* what you bring to the room.

And when you decide to walk? Do it without explanation.

Because the Real Girls way isn't about proving.

It's about *owning*.

Power Starts with One Brave Sentence: Featuring Ben Kiker, Executive Coach

"Silence isn't humility. It's often a habit we mistake for safety. But safety rarely leads to power, and power starts the minute you say something out loud that once scared you," says Ben Kiker (you'll remember him, he's the Silicon Valley–based performance and resilience coach who helps high achievers reframe their defining moments, regain momentum and set a practice for meaningful change).

Some of us were raised to believe speaking up made us "difficult." That asking for what we needed made us needy. That silence was grace and martyrdom was love. But guess what? Grace doesn't require swallowing your voice. And love? Real love? It can handle your full truth.

The moment you say the thing you've tiptoed around: "I'm not happy," "I want more," "This isn't working," your whole nervous system recalibrates. You stop whispering to survive and start speaking to *live*. That's when power begins. And it doesn't have to be loud. It just has to be yours.

5 Real Girls Questions I'd ask the legendary Bozoma Saint John about speaking up: Another abstract interview with intention.

Real Talk: If I could sit down with Boz, the marketing powerhouse, unapologetic truth-teller, and a woman who's redefined what power looks like in the C-suite, I'd bring five questions to the table. Why Boz? Because she doesn't just *talk* about owning power, she *embodies* it. She's bold, brilliant, loud when it matters, and quiet when it serves. She's reshaped how we see women in leadership—not by fitting in, but by standing the hell out.

Here's what I'd ask Boz:

1. What was the moment you realized your voice wasn't just valuable, it was non-negotiable? Was it in a boardroom? On a stage? After a loss? I want to know when she stopped softening the edges and started saying the thing out loud, even when it shook the room.

2. You once said on *The Real Housewives of Beverly Hills* that a boss told you that you "didn't have enough wins on the board." How did you decide that was the moment to walk away? Was it rage? Clarity? Exhaustion? I want to know what shifted in her body, her spirit, her gut. What voice inside finally said, "We're done here."

3. In the seasons of life when you've felt unseen or underestimated, especially in midlife, what do you tell yourself to keep showing up? Because we've all been there. Dismissed. Doubted. I want to know what internal dialogue she relies on to rise above the noise.

4. How do you decide when to speak up and when to let silence do the work? Women our age are often either silenced or expected to be the wise elder in the room. I want to hear how she navigates when to burn it down and when to walk out without a word.

5. What do you want your daughter, or the next generation of women, to know about speaking up before they're ready? Because most of us waited. Out of fear. Out of politeness. Out of survival. I want to know what Bozoma would say to help women stop waiting.

We Were Trained for Guilt, Not Agency:
Featuring Dr. Kimberly Sheridan, PhD

Why does prioritizing our own joy feel like breaking some sacred oath? Because for decades, we were groomed for guilt. From the birthday parties we planned to the emotions we swallowed, we were taught to carry the weight of everyone else's happiness, at the cost of our own. "We had to learn how to state our needs, but no one taught us how to act on them," says Kimberly Sheridan, PhD and Professor of Educational Psychology.

And when we finally *do* state them, our needs? That ache in our chest? That's not selfishness. That's generational programming. Guilt is what happens when a woman decides she's worthy in a system that taught her otherwise. "As long as I have some physical and mental ability, there's always the possibility for transformation," says Dr. Kimberly.

So, here's some truth: Agency is the new ambition.

Let that land. Because even when your hormones are haywire and your joints sound like a percussion section, you are *not* too late, too tired, or too far gone. I repeat: Agency is the new ambition. And reinvention doesn't require a roadmap, it just needs a refusal to shrink. Midlife isn't a flatline. It's a portal.

What I learned from the life-changing moments when I spoke up and stood out.

I've had a few important stand-up moments in my lifetime. For instance, the time I walked away from a good job because my boss asked me to lie. He wanted me to straight-up fabricate a budget line-item to cover for a decision that wasn't mine. I'd worked my ass off to earn trust, credibility, and integrity. And there I was, being asked to torch all three in a single email.

Another time? I refused to work on a project that went against everything I stand for, professionally, personally, and as a mom raising three sons. The project wasn't just misaligned, it was shady. It rewarded someone who hadn't earned it. And I couldn't reconcile putting my name on something that made me question my values.

What gave me the courage? Two things:

- The voice in my head that asked, "*Would you be OK if your boys watched this play out and saw you stay silent?*"
- The fire in my gut that said, "*You can lose a job, but don't lose yourself.*"

What did it feel like in my body?

Terrifying. Liberating. I could feel my pulse in my ears. My hands were steady, but my chest was tight. It felt like setting fire to a bridge I'd built with my own bare hands, knowing it was the only true way forward.

Final Takeaway

To the women still struggling to find their voice? Here's what I want you to know:

You don't owe anyone your silence. Not your boss. Not your partner. Not even your paycheck. If it makes you shrink, twist, or feel like you've got to explain away your integrity, *say the thing*. Even if your voice shakes. Even if your knees do, too.

Because every time you speak truth you remind yourself who the hell you are. And that voice? That's not just for you. It's for every woman watching who needs permission to do the same.

Say the thing.

Say it *for you*.

CHAPTER 9

Grieving Who You Were —
And Loving Who You Are

Loss doesn't always look like death or divorce. Sometimes it shows up in the form of someone else's opinion about your life, dressed up as "concern" or "just being honest."

As I talk to more and more Real Girls—friends, family, women I deeply admire—I keep uncovering layers I never fully appreciated or saw. Women who chose not to marry or have children, only to be met with smug pity or thinly veiled judgment.

Example: Not long ago I read an article by a woman who said she was once asked, "Did you forget to have kids?"

I mean... what in the actual fuck?

Some of us didn't follow the script: no rings, no kids, no white-picket bullshit. The world acted like we were defective appliances with missing parts. We've been told we're "missing out," or worse yet, treated like we don't matter because we didn't tick the boxes someone else drew in permanent marker.

Heads up: None of us are broken.

And then there are the fierce ones who decided to go it solo, who became mothers on their own terms in their 40s, only to face a wall of unsolicited opinions and not-so-subtle warnings from people who were supposed to be in their corner.

That kind of noise? It's its own kind of grief. You start carrying losses you didn't even know you had because someone else projected their story onto yours.

Real Girls Reality Check(list): How to grieve well, and defy its gravity to take on your next audacious adventure.

Real Talk: Grief isn't just for death. It's for versions of ourselves we outgrew, roles we clung to, dreams that aged out and people we thought would never leave. Here are some powerful quotes from insightful thinkers who have helped me reassess my relationship with my past selves and the woman I'm becoming.

Here's some food for thought:

"Grief is anything you lose that mattered—your body before babies, your marriage before resentment, your ambition before burnout."

—CLAIRE BIDWELL SMITH, Grief Therapist and Author of *Anxiety: The Missing Stage of Grief*

"We must let go of the life we have planned, so as to accept the one that is waiting for us."

—JOSEPH CAMPBELL, Author of *The Hero's Journey*

(continued)

"When we numb grief, we numb joy. You can't selectively numb."

—BRENÉ BROWN, from her book, *The Gifts of Imperfection*

"Death is not the opposite of life, but a part of it."

—ALUA ARTHUR, Death Doula and Founder of *Going With Grace*

"The woman I was at 30 would be shocked by the woman I am now. And honestly? I love that for her."

—JENNIFER, Real Girl, divorced, and freshly tattooed

How I found my true identity through multiple losses and love.

I've had my own seasons of loss.

In 2010, I lost my maternal grandmother, Gemma, six weeks after her lung cancer diagnosis (it happened Thanksgiving morning, no less). Just two days later, my stepmom Linda passed away from colon cancer at 56.

In just ten days.

Two women who shaped me.

Gone.

And if that wasn't enough, less than a week later I went into labor a month early and gave birth to my youngest son.

All of it—grief, birth, identity, mortality—hit at once.

Then there was the slow breakdown of my marriage. Letting go of that chapter meant saying goodbye not just to a relationship, but to the version of me I'd built around it: the wife, the family glue, the woman who stayed silent to keep things steady.

Losing that life gutted me. I didn't just grieve the marriage, in a way, I grieved the *me* I had become to survive it. But what shocked me more was the woman who emerged on the other side. I was bolder, clearer, and wiser. I found myself unwilling to shrink ever again. I was more fully *me* than ever before.

Then came love. Big, unexpected, wild, long-distance, logic-defying love I found with my Aussie Man. The kind that asked me to throw out every control mechanism I'd built to keep myself "safe."

I'd always been the woman with a plan, a spreadsheet, an exit strategy. I lived life braced for impact because the shoe *always* dropped, inevitably. And yet, I was the one who told him: *We don't need to have all the answers. Let's just see where this goes.*

And we did!

That moment? That was the tug-of-war–between who I'd been, the woman who needed certainty, and who I was becoming. The woman who chose uncertainty anyway because *this* love was worth the risk.

The urge to protect my kids, to not create more instability, was instinctively strong. But I also knew that if I kept living from fear, I'd never show them what it looks like to leap for joy, not just run from disaster.

These losses: the marriage, the women I loved, the younger, tightly-wound version of myself, stripped me bare. But they also gave me back something deeper, a self I'd buried under responsibility and survival. I stopped waiting to be ready, I started choosing what felt *real*.

So, if you're holding on too tight to the past, to the old version of you that kept you safe but now keeps you stuck, let this be your permission slip. The loss might shake you. But on the other side? You'll find a version of yourself that isn't just surviving.

You'll finally be free.

Spanx, subscriptions and surrendering the fantasy.

Which leads me to the Spanx Incident.

It was a few days before my 50th birthday and I was suiting up—*literally*—for my stepdaughter's wedding. I say "suiting up" because wrangling yourself into Spanx after 50 should count as a full-body CrossFit workout.

There I was in my bathroom, trying to squeeze 50 years of womanhood into a nylon-torture sausage casing marketed as "supportive." My left thigh slid in like a champ. The right? That bitch rebelled. Slippery with sweat and attitude. I did the hop, the shimmy, the silent scream.

Then came the boobs.

One tucked in obediently like it knew the drill.

The other just *refused*.

The packaging promised a "smooth silhouette." But what I had going was more like lumpy rage and a deep, existential crisis. I was sweating. I was swearing. I was seconds away from dislocating a rib. And then I looked in the mirror—red-faced, hair frizzed, one boob clearly out on strike—and thought: *I am way too old for this shit.*

Don't get me wrong. I wasn't too old to care. I was just too old to fight with my clothes to prove I still qualify as sexy or presentable. I'd spent decades chasing some fantasy version of myself, the woman who could wear thongs without screaming, survive on five hours of sleep and fresh air, and crush 12-hour days on the regular. She was cute. She was competent. But, she was tired. And if I'm honest? Maybe, just maybe, she wasn't ever really *me*.

These days, I'm done shapeshifting to make everyone else comfortable. The Spanx went in the trash. The dress looked great. And I danced all night, full-thighed, free-boobed, and unapologetically me.

Fast forward a few years. I'm no longer fighting my underwear, but I *am* fighting my inbox when an email pops up that nearly knocks the wind out of me.

Subject line: "Welcome to AARP!"

No warning. No foreplay. Just *"BAM! Congratulations, you've arrived!"* The official invitation to middle age. When that message landed, I remember thinking: *I still have a teenage kid in the house. I still get zits. I still Google the side effects of tequila. How the hell am I eligible for senior discounts?*

And yet, I clicked to learn more.

I didn't sign up that day. But I *did* read the whole thing like it was the final chapter of a spy thriller. Cruise deals? Tempting. Rx discounts? Suddenly sexy. Magazine subscriptions I used to roll my eyes at? Now, they all felt like survival guides. It was humbling. It was surreal. It was stupidly funny.

And yeah, I signed up. Proudly. No shame, no hesitation, just me and my shiny new AARP card asking every cashier within a 10-mile radius, "Y'all do the discount?"

Because listen, I may be aging, but I am *not* dumb. Saving money is hot. So is owning your stage of life like a raging coupon queen.

These moments, my thong funeral pyre, the shapewear breakdown, the AARP welcome mat, they aren't about age so much as they are about *reality*. About finally accepting that our bodies, priorities, and standards are shifting in real time whether we like it or not.

The big lesson here is that acceptance isn't defeat. It's permission:
To take off the Spanx.
To ignore that email.
To wear full-ass briefs and still feel hot.
To say, "No thanks, Tom Hanks" to performative beauty standards and, "Yes, please" to comfort, joy and ease.

This chapter of life isn't about holding on to who you were. It's about honoring who you've become and deciding what (and who) still fits. The day I stopped waging war with my underwear and started laughing at my inbox was the day I felt more like myself than I had in years.

Expert Q&A with Diane Heiler: Widowed Author, Poet, And Unfiltered Voice For Reinvention.

Diane Heiler writes real. Her memoir, *A Widow's Fire: An Intimate Memoir of Heartbreak, Survival, and Moving On,* chronicles how she reconstructed her life after losing her husband of 25 years (together for 29). And then surprised everyone, including herself, by falling in love again at age 80. No fluff. No filter. Just truth.

Q: What did people most misunderstand about your grief—and what did you really need to hear in the early days?

A: *Everyone told me to "buck up." Even before he died, people said, "He'll get better." But the doctor was honest: "I can buy you time—but there's no cure." I collapsed. I had no roadmap. My kids had their own lives. I withdrew, wrote poetry, and cried until I didn't recognize the woman emerging. Two years later—and the grief is still real.*

Q: You speak so plainly about caregiving's emotional toll. What's the most important thing women need to know?

A: *You must prioritize yourself. I told my kids this, but they swore I always put them first. But I didn't. I needed to take care of me— otherwise, I couldn't care for anyone. After he passed, I went up to our mountain home, broke down, and wrote my way through it. That self-love kept me alive.*

Q: How did you reinvent your identity—not as a wife or widow, but simply as Diane?

A: *There's a difference between divorce and widowhood. Divorce gets side-eye. Widowhood gets casseroles—but both hurt. I still get mail for my husband. I don't need reminders, I'm doing the work. The greatest gift I gave myself was learning to like myself—fully and unfiltered. Confidence changes you. You walk into a room owning yourself—and that is beautiful, at any age.*

Q: What boundary did you need most after his death—and how did people react?

A: *When friends dropped in, I couldn't face them. I'd say, "I'm sorry, I can't." I needed space. Two months in, my husband's best friend told me, "Get out of the damn house. Go live." I did—and I fell in love again. At 80. And yes, it surprised me: sex still happens. I researched and discovered it's totally natural. Some women resisted the topic, but men thanked me for bringing it up. I say it loud: Passion doesn't fade with age.*

Q: What's the permission slip you'd hand every woman in midlife, in big, bold letters?

A: *Love yourself first. Then love the world. And have a damn blast going down doing it. This is your time. Live it like you mean it.*

How (and why) to strip the veneer off your life and say what you really think.

There's no "easy" button for any of this. I *still* catch myself trying to script the version of me other people get to see. You know, the "nice" one. The "quiet" one. The "peacekeeper" who smiles through the bullshit and brings gluten-free muffins to the meeting she wasn't invited to.

I used to think if I could just stay small enough, agreeable enough, low maintenance enough, maybe I'd earn my spot at the table or at least not get kicked out of the room.

So, I did a lot of swallowing:
My opinions.
My anger.
My truth.
And, yeah, a *ton* of other shit. Served up with a side of forced grace and a lukewarm glass of "I'm fine."

Why? Because I thought that shrinking made me lovable. Turns out it just made me smaller. Letting go of attempted perfection wasn't some slow-mo, wind-in-my-hair, music-swelling, power-blazer moment. It was messy. Uneven. Like ripping off a too-tight bra in a Target parking lot (yes, I've done it many times). It was awkward, overdue, and absolutely necessary.

Maybe a better analogy is that it felt like peeling off a pair of Spanx after sweating through someone else's expectations all day—sticky, undignified, and slightly dangerous if done too fast. But underneath all that control-freakery? There I was, loud, honest, fully uncorked.

These days, I don't contort myself to be digestible. I say the thing. I wear the thing. I ask for what I want. And guess what? The world hasn't ended yet.

Here's the deal, Real Girl to Real Girl:

- Stop editing yourself to fit inside someone else's comfort zone.
- You're not here to be liked. You're here to be true.
- If the real you makes some people squirm? In the immortal words of Mel Robbins: Let them.

You're not too much. You're finally just enough.

Real Girls on Letting Go, Leveling Up and Loving Who They Are Now

Midlife grief isn't always wrapped in black dresses and casseroles. Sometimes it shows up in the mirror when you barely recognize the woman staring back. Sometimes it's the sound of silence in a house that used to be full. And sometimes it's the sacred unraveling of a life you outgrew—even if it was one you once begged for.

"It's OK to mourn the person you once were," says Dr. Nivedita Nayak, a Clinical Psychologist who's spent more than 15 years walking women through the identity earthquakes of midlife. "We're told to stay youthful, stay busy, stay grateful—but rarely are we encouraged to grieve what we've lost."

Whether that's the loss of mothering young children, a shifted career identity, faded friendships, or a body that feels foreign, Dr. Nayak reminds us that grief doesn't mean you're broken—it means you're human.

This isn't just about menopause or wrinkles. It's about a deep, internal shedding. "One patient told me, 'It's like I'm living in my own body, but I don't recognize myself anymore,'" she recalls. Midlife, she says, is less about decline and more about reckoning—a necessary pause between the past you and the new one trying to emerge.

What makes these transitions even harder? The old family roles we never realized we were still playing. As LFMT, Charlie Bauman explains: "Most of us operate from unconscious blueprints laid down in childhood—caretaker, peacemaker, fixer, achiever. Even if those roles don't serve us anymore, we cling to them because, well, they're familiar. It's what we know."

And when we finally start to act outside the expectations of our family system? Let's just say the applause is... not immediate. "When women begin to behave in new and different ways, out of accordance with family norms, they receive scrutiny and judgment," says Charlie. "That shame hits hard—because they're not just breaking a habit, they're disrupting an entire generational pattern."

Dr. Nayak calls this *sacred tension*: the push-pull between mourning and becoming. "When we honor what we've lost," she says, "we also make room for what's still unfolding."

And that? That's where power begins.

Here's How Some Real Girls Are Walking That Line:

- After two divorces and a transatlantic reset, Jennifer moved in with her mother and found healing in the small, everyday routines: morning coffee, shared TV time, the comfortable silence of cohabitating with someone who gets you. "I needed her as much as she needed me," says Jennifer. "She became my world, and I was her favorite—not because I was better, but because I was *her*."

  Now? She's missing her mother, her purpose, and her mirror, but finding meaning in different places. "I finally stopped looking for validation in someone else's reflection." But she's not trying to fill the hole—she's learning to honor it. This time, she's calling out the habit so many of us took decades to break—becoming whoever the person we're dating needs us to be. "It took a lot of bad experiences to realize I'm happiest on my own," she says. "There's nothing wrong with being a loner. There's nothing wrong with me."

  According to Charlie, this kind of shape-shifting is classic female socialization: "Girls are raised to accommodate, adjust, and be likable. So, when we finally prioritize ourselves, it can feel selfish. But that's not guilt—it's freedom dressed in discomfort."

- While separating from her partner and her financial identity, Riley was also launching a culturally-rooted business for her children. "Starting my business while divorcing? Messy, overwhelming, empowering as hell," says Riley, an entrepreneur. She had no net, no guarantee. Just guts. "I invested everything, emotionally and financially, into building a life I actually believed in." What her kids saw? A woman who didn't shrink, and a mom who took full ownership of her life, even when it was hard.

- After decades working in the entertainment world and living in government housing, Gloria, an Empowerment Coach and Professional Singer, didn't have a financial portfolio. But she did have one thing money can't buy, a life full of artistic meaning. "I followed a soulful path," she says. Then, later in life, with a new partner and a fresh sense of purpose, she became debt-free, then unstoppable. "I didn't chase wealth, but I found power anyway." Now? She coaches women to thrive beyond 40. Her favorite lesson: "Abundance isn't just about income. It's about reclaiming your voice and choosing a future that feels like freedom."

What I saw in the mirror and how it moved me from grief to self-love.

One day not too long ago, I looked in the mirror and came to terms with all of these things:

- Wrinkles where there used to be smoothness.
- A stomach that's lived, stretched, birthed, and battled stress.
- Hands that look alarmingly like my mother's.
- Eyelids folding in on themselves like they're trying to quit the job.

And underneath all of that? A woman who worked her ass off. Built a life from scratch. Raised a crew of humans. Weathered heartbreak, divorce and career landmines. Not to mention parenting adult kids who sometimes forget you're not a punching bag.

Which leads me to: My bikini moment. Cue the deep breath and full-body reckoning.

We were planning a trip to Sicily, me and my Aussie Man, and I ordered this delicious navy-blue bikini. Just the bikini. No backup one-piece, no "just in case" Amazon panic buy. Just this cute little two-piece that whispered: *"You've still got it, babe."*

I'd worn this same bikini the summer before and felt pretty darn good.

But this year? I was nervous. Not for any specific reason. I just had a vague, creeping, mid-50s feeling like my body had changed and no one had bothered to send me the memo. When the bikini arrived, I was a full-blown mess.

In preparation, I work out. I plank. I do the deep-core stuff. I try not to eat like a raccoon in an empty gas station. I've earned my semi-toned, strong-as-hell body. And still, that tiny bikini felt like it carried the weight of all my years.

I put it on anyway. And stood there. Turning. Assessing. One boob slightly lower than the other. Yes, even post-boob job, gravity's a petty bitch. Stomach looking like I'd skipped moisturizer for, I don't know, a decade. And my ass? Still cute, I'm told, thanks to the squats. But maybe a little less defiant in those bottoms than I remembered.

I didn't hate what I saw. But I wasn't instantly strutting, either.

It wasn't a "*Yay, me!*" moment. It was a "*Shit, this is me*" moment. And for a split second, I thought: "*Am I too old for this shit?*" Then something in me snapped. Not a dramatic, Instagram-worthy "love yourself" awakening. More like a fed-up, stompy toddler throwing down her juice box. I said out loud, probably to my reflection but also maybe to every woman who's ever doubted herself in a dressing room: "Fuck that noise. I'm wearing the bikini."

Because here's what I *also* saw:

A woman who has earned her skin.

A woman with stories.

A woman who's taken the hits (divorce, grief, gut-punches life didn't warn her about) and still shows up with a banging ass (again, I'm told), a backbone of steel, and a heart that refuses to quit.

Final Takeaway

So, for the women reading this who are standing in front of your mirror, wrestling with grief over the girl you were (and disbelief over the woman staring back at you now), hear me when I say this:

You don't owe youthfulness to anyone. You don't need permission to take up space. You don't have to earn confidence with perfection. You just have to decide you're enough—wrinkles, wobbles, wisdom and all.

And if that voice in your head ever whispers, *"Maybe you should cover up..."*

You have every right to say back: "Watch me walk in like I own the damn beach."

5 Real Girls Reflections About Grief:
A worksheet for a real midlife badass.

Grief is gritty. Growth is glorious. And you? You're still unfolding. Let the tears come, let the laughter in and don't forget, loving who you are now doesn't mean abandoning who you were. It means honoring her by becoming everything she never thought possible. So, with those words in mind, here's a handful of questions to ask yourself as you ponder your relationship with grief:

1. What part of you are you still grieving—and why?
2. What have you let go of that once defined you?
3. What's something about aging that surprised you—in a good way?
4. Who do you feel closest to now that you've shifted?
5. What advice would you give your past self?

CHAPTER 10

Hormones, Sex and The What-The-F*ck Years

Here's a thing that no one told me about midlife: It's not just your hormones that bail, it's your sense of sexual identity. One minute I felt sexy, alive, curious. The next, I wasn't sure I'd ever feel anything again except mildly irritated. There's pelvic-floor sabotage. Non-existent orgasms. The crying-over-tile-samples phase. And full-body heat waves that show up like uninvited houseguests.

And that's just part of the fun.

After my divorce, and right around the time menopause came crashing through like a drunk cousin at a wedding, I bought my first vibrator, the one I mentioned way back in Chapter 1 (we've come a long way, girl). I was in my *late 40s*. Let that marinate.

It arrived in one of those "discreet" boxes, like I'd ordered a crime scene cleanup kit. I opened it cautiously, half-expecting it to hum on its own. I wasn't new to sex, but I was brand new to asking myself what I liked. And the truth? I didn't know.

Worse still, I had to admit something I had never said out loud, not even to myself until my mid-50s: I had never really had many orgasms. And the ones I had? Not from penetration. Not from connection. Not from understanding my own body.

That realization hit like a gut punch. How had I gone this long without understanding my own pleasure? How had I spent decades being agreeable, going along, faking it, waiting for it to be over, or just … numb?

And now, just as I was starting to get comfortable with wanting something more, real pleasure, real intimacy, real *fucking orgasms*, my desire up and disappeared. Not dramatically. Just … gone. Like it slipped out the backdoor with my metabolism and my tolerance for bullshit.

Then came the bladder issues. Because nothing says "let's get it on" like worrying you might go pee mid-thrust. Sexy, right? Intimacy became less about connection and more about logistics. Planning. Padding. Overthinking. Sometimes, full-on avoidance. The confusion that followed? Brutal.

How do you tell someone you love: "I finally figured out how to get there, and now I'm not sure I even want to try"? How do you admit that sex feels like a setup for disappointment or worse, like your vagina might throw a protest? I had friends describe sex post-50 like "sandpaper in a sock" or "a haunted house with all the lights on." One friend straight-up said, "At least your vagina isn't broken."

And I was like, *Define broken, babe?*

Because mine feels more like a vintage appliance—high maintenance, prone to leaks, and not compatible with modern power sources. But here's what I've realized and what no one said clearly enough: This isn't just *my* story.

"A broken vagina is a vagina that has lost all its moisture and flexibility," my friend Steph told me. "It's like a million glass shards up in there when we're having sex." What she was describing is what physicians call "vaginal atrophy" which is a reference to dead vaginal tissues. But for Steph it wasn't just the pain and lack of lubrication, it was an absolute lack of desire, too.

❦

"I think the thing we need to reframe is the desire part—how do I want it? This is the hardest part for me," she says, "I love my husband and he's worth the effort, but I really have to make an effort." Steph did the research around HRT, testosterone, and estradiol pills, and found a few different options, including an internal laser treatment (oof!). But she had to seek out a menopausal specialist for testosterone because her own OB/GYN wouldn't prescribe it. "I just started testosterone, and I've seen minimal uptick in desire but I'm just getting started, so the jury is still out."

Do you see it? It's a pattern. It's the married women quietly faking it because they don't know how to start the conversation. It's the single women wondering if their window closed without warning. It's the queer women relearning their own desire in bodies that no longer respond the way they used to. It's the bi women navigating layers of identity, expectation, and biology all at once. We've all been handed the same silent script:

Don't ask too many questions.

Don't want too much.

Don't talk about it when it stops working.

But, I'm done whispering. Because one day I saw a chart in the book *All Fours* by Miranda July.

One chart. Two lines.

Estrogen for women? A dramatic cliff dive.

Testosterone for men? A lazy river.

And for the first time, it all *clicked*. The lack of desire. The bladder drama. The quiet grief over a body I never fully understood.

That chart didn't fix me. It freed me. It gave me language, and language gave me power, not to go back, but to move forward without shame. Because I'm not broken, I'm just newly honest. And if you're here, too, figuring it out late, navigating the weird, rewiring your desires—you're not alone.

You're not late. Once again, you're right on time.

And you deserve everything: good, messy, curious, and the real that's still to come.

Let's Get One Thing Straight: Midlife sex isn't dead—it's just getting rewritten.

They told us menopause was the end of our sexual prime, but they forgot to mention that for a lot of us it's finally the beginning. Let's be real: midlife sex can be confusing, painful, elusive—or shockingly better than ever. So, whether you're grieving lost desire, discovering a new relationship with your body, or just sick of faking it, this chapter is your permission slip to ask for more, explore more, and say "hell no" to one-size-fits-all intimacy advice.

Here are five truths I wish someone had screamed at me from a podium (or whispered to me over wine) a decade ago:

1.   Painful sex isn't normal, it's just common (and fixable).

Dr. Mary Claire Haver, OB/GYN and Menopause Specialist, calls out genitourinary syndrome of menopause (GSM) as the silent saboteur of midlife sex. Burning, dryness, and tearing isn't just "getting older," it's treatable. You are not broken. You need lube, a provider who listens, and possibly a prescription.

"There's no badge of honor for suffering through painful sex. Advocate for your comfort. Your pleasure is not optional."

—DR. MARY CLAIRE HAVER, *The New Menopause*

2.   Desire isn't dead, it's just not on a timer anymore.

Author of *Come As You Are*, Dr. Emily Nagoski, breaks down responsive vs. spontaneous desire. At midlife many of us don't feel horny out of nowhere—and that's *normal*. Desire often follows arousal. Translation: Start the engine before deciding on the destination.

"Pleasure is the measure. Not performance. Not frequency. Just joy."

—DR. EMILY NAGOSKI

3. You're not the only one who's never had an orgasm.

Enter Heather Corinna, Queer Midlife Icon and Author of *What Fresh Hell Is This?* Their writing unapologetically names the shame so many of us carry, especially if we've been faking pleasure for decades. This is your invitation to unlearn the performance and explore what *you* like, even if you're 58 and holding a vibrator for the first time.

"You deserve curiosity, not comparison."   —HEATHER CORINNA

4. Solo sex isn't second best, it's smart, sexy self-care.

Midlife intimacy expert Dr. Shannon Chavez reminds us that masturbation is a crucial part of hormonal health, pelvic floor recovery and libido confidence. Solo time builds body literacy and lets you explore without performance pressure. And yes, it counts as sex. Maybe better.

"Your body is not a stranger. Say hello."   —DR. SHANNON CHAVEZ

5. Intimacy is more than orgasms, it's feeling seen.

Sex Therapist Vanessa Marin, in *Sex Talks: The Five Conversations That Will Transform Your Love Live*, which she co-wrote with her husband, reminds us that intimacy isn't just heat or bodies, it's showing up. Real intimacy is waking up the courage to be seen and letting someone in, again and again.

"Real intimacy is about making the choice to be vulnerable, over and over again."
—VANESSA MARIN

The "What's wrong with me?" spiral and the truth that finally released me.

Was there a moment I felt broken?

Absolutely. And not in the dramatic, Lifetime movie way. It was more like a slow, creeping erosion, where one day you wake up and realize your body, your desire, your very sense of self has quietly left the chat.

It came on slowly. No fireworks. No fancy exit. Just a barely noticeable fade-out, like a dimmer switch someone kept twisting a little bit lower every day. One minute I had a pulse for pleasure. The next? I was mentally reviewing my to-do list mid-makeout.

And here's the truth I only recently owned: *Pleasure*—real, electric, mine—was never actually a thing for me. Before menopause, I thought of it like the smoke alarm battery, something that would start beeping eventually, but not my problem until it did. I didn't ask questions. I didn't even *know* I was missing anything. I just did what good girls do: stayed quiet, performed well, pressed on.

I faked orgasms I hadn't even given myself permission to want. I didn't know what turned me on. I didn't know how to ask. And honestly? I didn't even know *I could*. It wasn't until post-divorce, right at the start of menopause, that I had my first real come-to-Jesus moment, with myself and *that* vibrator that nearly got me flagged by the TSA. It was humbling. And a little hilarious. But mostly? It was sobering.

Because I had lived an entire life without really knowing how I worked. And once I finally started to figure it out: what I liked, what I didn't, how to get off in a way that didn't feel like theater, it all started slipping through my fingers again. First came the low desire. Then the bladder stuff. Then the total confusion and panic. And the worst part? I didn't know how to talk about it. Not to myself. Not to my partner.

There was a morning (Sunday, soft and quiet) where we were lying in bed with coffee. I decided to try, I didn't have the right words, but I had to *try*. Because the silence was starting to feel louder than anything else. I told him the truth: I didn't feel broken *by him* or *because of us*. But I felt broken *in me*. And I didn't know how to fix it. Or even *if* it could be fixed.

It was an incredibly difficult conversation. I cried, I rambled, I reached for metaphors that made no sense. But he listened, and that mattered. A lot. Somewhere in the aftermath of that conversation I picked up *Come As You Are* by Dr. Emily Nagoski, and her words hit like an unvarnished truth to my soul:

"You are normal. Your body is not a machine; it's a living system. And desire is not a light switch—it's a garden. You have to tend to it."

That line? That garden metaphor? It tore something open in me. I had been trying to force my desire to show up like a scheduled guest. But it needed sunlight. Care. Curiosity. It needed me to stop treating it like a malfunctioning iPhone app and start honoring it like something sacred and alive.

And in that messy, quiet moment, coffee in one hand, confusion in the other, I remembered something I already knew:

I'm not alone.

This experience isn't rare. In fact, it's common. *Ridiculously* common. And yet we carry it like a secret shame. Married women. Single women. Women who love women. Women who love both. So many of us pretend our pleasure isn't relevant or real or pretend we *understand* it when we never actually got the download in the first place.

And yeah, maybe I got to the realization party a little late (I blame my tardiness on a wandering attention span and group-chat rabbit holes). But I got there. I'm still getting there.

One thing I know for sure: Shame thrives in silence. And silence is where pleasure goes to die.

So here I am, breaking the silence, one brutally honest book chapter, coffee-fueled convo and post-menopausal vibrator saga at a time.

The Other Side Of Menopause—A Sexy Awakening:
Featuring Dr. Trina Read, Canadian Sexologist
& Author of *Sex Boot Camp*

What if your sexiest chapter isn't behind you—it's actually just getting started? Dr. Trina Read has spent 25 years helping women in long-term relationships rewrite the rules of intimacy. Her take? After 50, women stop tending and mending everyone else and finally start prioritizing themselves. And guess what happens? They get clearer about what they want and bolder about asking for it.

"It's realistic to say that a woman in her 50s or beyond hits her sexual stride and becomes the sexiest version of herself. The problem? Society tells her the door has closed. And too many women believe it."

Dr. Trina's insight? Younger women often struggle to lean into pleasure or ask for what they want. But something shifts after 50. Confidence grows. Inhibitions drop. Sensuality steps forward. Sex becomes less about the "ta-da" moment and more about a toe-curling, three-dimensional experience.

And the stats back her up: a 2023 AARP study found that 83% of people over 40 still have erotic fantasies—and that sexual activity like masturbation and oral sex increases after 50. Of course, it's not always easy. More than a third of women in menopause report sexual difficulties. Estrogen drops. Desire shifts. Orgasms don't show up on cue.

But Dr. Trina says that's not the end of pleasure—it's the beginning of new conversations.

To reignite pleasure at this stage, women need to talk about:

- Their changed bodies.
- Their shifting desire patterns (yes, even daily).
- Their need for something different during sex.

Dr. Trina's advice? Stay curious. Stay positive. And stay loud about your needs. The key to great sex after 50 isn't trying to get back to your 20s—it's evolving into something richer, slower, and a whole lot deeper. "Your 60s can be your most sensual decade," she says. "The trick is to keep a positive mindset through the turbulence of your 40s and 50s—and let that pleasure bloom."

From numb to nuclear: The exact second I chose me.

Post-divorce, in my mid-40s, I didn't exactly feel like a sexual powerhouse. I felt invisible. Like a human leftovers bin—half-used, half-healed—and barely in the mood for anything that required more than sweatpants and lip balm.

Then one day, over coffee, a friend casually mentioned that her "new BFF" was her detachable shower head. She said it with a laugh, but it landed like a dare. I couldn't stop thinking about it. Not because I was turned on, but because I was *curious*. What if that worked for *me*? What if I could finally figure out something I'd somehow skipped entirely?

Because here's the truth: I hadn't had many orgasms in my life. And none—zero—from penetration. Pleasure had always felt like a long-lost lover I barely knew. Not someone I'd ever really invited over.

So, I decided to try.

Home alone one night I stepped into the shower, turned up the pressure, angled the nozzle and *holy shit*. It wasn't dramatic or cinematic. But it was *real*. Electric. Warm. Focused. And mine. No partner. No performance. No pretending. I stood there afterward—wet, naked, wide-eyed—and for the first time in a long time, I felt powerful. Not because I had *done* something miraculous, but because I had finally *owned* it.

It wasn't about an orgasm. It was about ownership. Ownership of my body, of my desire. Of the simple fact that I mattered, not as someone's partner, or caretaker, or supporting actress, but as a woman with her own pleasure map, even if I was just now sketching it out in pencil.

I also felt a pang of grief. For all the years I didn't know this, for the younger me who stayed quiet, didn't ask, didn't know how. For the sex I had that was fine, but not *mine*.

A few days later, I came across *that* chart again, the one I mentioned earlier from Miranda July's *All Fours*. I remembered the two lines:

Estrogen crashing for women.

Testosterone coasting for men.

That simple visual was a gut punch and a permission slip all at once. Because suddenly it all made sense. I wasn't broken. I was just late to the party. Late to the language. Late to the ownership. But I got there.

And if you're sitting there reading this thinking: "*Me too.*"

You're not late, you're ready.

Expert Q&A with Annette Benedetti: Sex & Intimacy Coach, Host of *Talk Sex with Annette*

On the hunt for clarity, we called in for some no-BS wisdom from Annette Benedetti, a sex and intimacy coach and host of *Talk Sex with Annette*. She's here to dismantle the myths, rewrite the script and remind you that midlife isn't a dry spell, it's an awakening. Grab your lube, your journal, or your favorite toy, and let's go there:

Q: Midlife hit and so did the disappearing act on my libido. What's actually going on—and how do I get the spark back without faking it?

A: *Your hormones may be shifting, but your desire didn't ghost you— it just stopped showing up for half-assed sex. The fast-pass to arousal you used to rely on? It might not work anymore. And maybe that's a gift. Because for many of us, it never delivered real, embodied* *pleasure anyway. Midlife blows the doors off the performance stage. It says: No more people-pleasing, no more faking it, no more chasing the 20-something version of sexy. Now? It's about discovering what truly turns you on. From hormone therapy to a reawakening of your erotic power, the spark is still there. You just have to stop looking for it in the same damn place.*

Q: What about women who *want* intimacy but feel betrayed by their bodies—painful sex, dryness, zero interest?

A: *Let's be clear: Painful sex is not your new normal. It's your body yelling, "Not like this." And she deserves better. Midlife sex needs new tools—think pelvic floor therapy, vaginal estrogen, and a serious rewrite of what intimacy means. Because penetration isn't the gold standard. It never was. Reclaim your pleasure with curiosity and zero apology. Lube is great, but so is foreplay that lasts longer than a commercial break. Redefine intimacy on your terms. Slow down. Feel everything. And throw the old sex script in the trash.*

Q: What sex myths need to be torched once and for all?

A: *Annette calls bullshit on these tropes:*

- *"Sex gets boring with time." Nah. It gets boring when we stop evolving.*
- *"Menopause = sex is over." False. It's the start of your wildest chapter—if you let it be.*
- *"If the spark fades, love is dead." Nope. The spark fades when no one feeds it. Get creative.*
- *"Midlife women aren't sexy." Lie. We're magnetic when we stop chasing approval and start owning our bodies.*
- *"Being wanted = being sexy." Wrong. Wanting yourself? That's the real power move.*

Q: Why does reclaiming sexual pleasure matter outside the bedroom?

A: *Because when you reclaim your pleasure, you reclaim your power.*

You stop waiting to be chosen. You start living lit up, from your bedroom to your boardroom. Pleasure isn't indulgent, it's information. When you follow what excites you, you build boundaries, ambition, and joy. That's sovereignty.

Q: Where should a woman start if she doesn't even know what she wants anymore?
A: *Start where it feels safest, your body, your heart, your vibrator. You don't need a plan. You need presence. Touch yourself without a goal. Listen to what your body misses. Grieve the versions of you that only knew how to give. And when you're ready, follow what feels good. It's all yours.*

Real intimacy? It starts way before the bedroom.

Over the years I've learned that intimacy isn't about the sex.

Not really.

Not just.

Not always.

Intimacy isn't a waxed bikini and a perfect orgasm on command. It's not lingerie that itches or some bullshit *Cosmopolitan* magazine tip about ice cubes and whipped cream. It's not performative moaning or being "low maintenance" so someone else feels comfortable. Here's what I know now, deep in my bones (and hips and bladder):

True intimacy is when someone reaches for your hand, not your ass, when you're crying so hard your nose is running and your mascara looks like a Rorschach test. Other times it's the early Sunday morning coffee in bed when you finally whisper to your partner what you couldn't name for weeks, that your desire has faded and you don't know why and you're scared it might not come back. That your bladder's betraying you. That sex, in all its glory, sometimes feels like broken glass. That you're grieving the part of you that used to ache with wanting.

And it's that person looking at you—not with pity, not with panic but with soft eyes and an "OK, let's figure this out together."

That's intimacy.

It's laughter during sex when your leg cramps mid-thrust. It's silence that doesn't need to be filled. It's a partner who asks, "Do you want me to grab you a coffee?" and brings it anyway even when you say no. It's feeling safe enough to admit that you're just now learning what turns you on.

Sometimes it's a showerhead you bought yourself. A vibrator you almost accidentally packed in your carry-on (OK, or maybe I did pack?). A journal entry where you finally write down, "I've never had an orgasm from penetration and I'm done pretending."

Reality is not always pretty. But God, it's real. So no, they didn't teach us this in our 20s but they should have. Instead, they gave us rom-coms, rules and warnings. They told us to be chill, be hot, be good, be grateful. But now? Now we know. Intimacy is choosing to stay. Not just with a partner, with yourself. In all your sweaty, leaky, glorious midlife magic. And if you need a reminder? This is it.

You're not broken. You're becoming.

This Isn't the End of Your Sex Life, It's the Reboot: Featuring Dr. Trina Read, Canadian Sexologist; and Dr. Elizabeth Franze, Pelvic Floor Therapist & Sex Counselor

Menopause doesn't kill your sex life. Silence does. Too many women are left in the dark, sidelined by vaginal dryness, disappearing libido, pain during sex, and a pile of emotional shame that makes them question if it's all just... over.

It's not.

Dr. Trina Read, whom you'll remember from earlier in this chapter, spent over two decades helping women in long-term relationships rekindle intimacy, says midlife can be a full-blown sexy awakening. Why? Because when your oxytocin dips (the tending-and-mending hormone), you finally stop mothering the world and start prioritizing yourself. "Women in their 50s can hit their sexual stride and become the sexiest version of themselves, not in spite of aging, but because of it," she says.

Meanwhile, Dr. Elizabeth Franze is in the trenches with women whose bodies don't feel like their own anymore. Through pelvic floor therapy, breathwork, and nervous system regulation, she helps women feel safe again in their skin and unlock the kind of pleasure that comes from deep connection and understanding. "Pleasure starts with safety," she explains, "And once women reconnect with their bodies, sex becomes richer, slower, more grounded. More real."

So, what can help?

- Vaginal estrogen
- Pelvic floor therapy
- Better lube
- Slower build-up
- Less pressure
- More curiosity
- Conversations that don't start with "sorry."

And let's name what no one taught us how to say out loud:

- My body feels different.
- I need more time.
- I don't want the kind of sex we used to have.
- I want something new.

This season of life isn't about shrinking back or pushing through.

It's about asking for what you want, and leaning into the pleasure that's still yours to claim. "Intimacy doesn't fade with age," Dr. Franze reminds us, "It transforms." For emphasis, Dr. Read adds, "And it can be mind-blowing if we stop chasing the sex we had at 20 and start honoring the pleasure we want now."

Midlife sex isn't a throwback. It's a revolution.

Honestly, what does "good in bed" even mean?

I used to think being "good in bed" meant being a low-maintenance, perfectly waxed, orgasm-on-demand kind of woman. You know, the ones I imagined my friends were. The ones I saw in rom-coms or talked to at dinner parties, the women who winked when someone said "multiple" or made some offhand comment about needing a "recharge" after a weekend away with their husband.

In my head these women were effortlessly hot. Effortlessly responsive. Effortlessly confident. They packed lingerie without anxiety. Moaned without overthinking it. Knew what they liked. Knew how to ask for it. And always, *always* seemed to want it. I built them into gods. Shrines. The sex version of Pinterest boards—curated and sparkling and utterly unattainable.

Meanwhile, I was faking it. The orgasms, the enthusiasm, the comfort in my own skin. I played the role, hit the cues, made the right sounds. But every day I did fake it, doing so chipped away at me a little more. I wasn't just pretending in bed—I was pretending in life. Pretending I knew what pleasure meant. Pretending I was normal, pretending I wasn't broken. Until I finally stopped pretending.

Not because of him or for him. But because of me. Because post-divorce, post-menopause, post-trying-to-be-who-I-thought-I-should-be, I met someone when I had finally started becoming who I actually *was*.

My Aussie Man didn't "fix" anything. But he made space. He listened. He asked questions. He didn't expect me to perform. And that gave me permission to get honest with him and, more importantly, with myself. Yes, the orgasms came late. So did the curiosity. So did the confidence. But they came.

Turns out, I wasn't the only one who didn't know her own body. I wasn't the only one who never had an orgasm from penetration. I wasn't the only one who thought she was broken. It turns out she was just never taught how to ask for what she needed. And no, it didn't happen in my 20s. Or my 30s. Or even my 40s. But it happened. And it's still happening. I'm still learning. Still laughing. Still figuring it out.

5 Permission Slips for Midlife Sex

Midlife sex isn't less. It's more: more honest, more grounded, more *you*. You don't owe anyone a performance. You owe yourself pleasure, curiosity and truth. Welcome to the WTAF years. They're wild. They're wise. And they're all yours.

- You can say no and still love your body.
- You can say yes to new things (alone or with someone else).
- You can explore kink or remain vanilla with zero apologies.
- You can take breaks—and come back when you're ready.
- You can ask for what you want, even if it's just eye contact and a nap.

Final Takeaway

These days, "good in bed" means I get to show up fully. I get to say *yes* when I want to and no when I don't. And I no longer perform. I *participate*.

The highlight reel I made up in my head? That was never real. But *this*? This tangled, raw, midlife sexual becoming with a sex drive that now shows up late, unshowered and asking what's for dinner? This is the real flex. Not because everything works perfectly, but because *I* finally do. Even when my libido pulls a no-show, I still show the hell up, for my body, my pleasure, and myself.

No shame. No filters. Just truth, lube and full ownership.

This is real. And it's mine.

CHAPTER 11

Wills, Trusts, and All That Jazz

I never had just one singular *"Oh hell!"* moment that made me realize I needed to face my mountain of end-of-life paperwork. There were hundreds of them.

They were like grief bombs on delay. When my stepmother and grandmother died two days apart while I was eight months pregnant with my third son, those losses shattered me. My heart was bleeding, yet I was still expected to function as if nothing had changed.

That's when it hit me, hard and loud: Death doesn't wait. Life doesn't pause. And leaving your shit unhandled isn't an option anymore. I was suddenly the adult in charge of someone else's chaos, and I knew I didn't want to leave that same mess behind for my kids.

But honestly, the unraveling started way before that. My mom was a young, fierce single mother who worked her ass off. Without even saying it, she taught me that security is earned, not gifted. And that you never, ever rely on someone else to give it to you.

That message got baked into my bones. Scarcity became a lifestyle and a shield. I hustled, saved every cent, and gave up my dream Toyota 4Runner I had bought for myself because I convinced my dad I needed to sell it. In exchange he gave me a less shiny, salvaged car with no payment.

Practical? Sure. But that trade stung.

I bought my first house with $7000 I scraped together, and as you might remember, I stocked the silverware drawer with nothing but knives because all I could afford to eat were peanut butter and jelly sandwiches.

I made it work. I always made it work. But every decision came with one haunting question: If it all falls apart, can I survive this alone? Then came the divorce. The paperwork. All the legal shit.

Not to mention the reality of finally earning real money in my career, and knowing I needed to write it all down (wills, trusts, everything) hit me hard. I needed to do it because I had three sons and no interest in turning my death into a scavenger hunt. No more avoidance. No more "someday." I had to handle my business.

And then I met my Aussie Man.

Love. Partnership. Planning for a future that wasn't just about me anymore. We saved. We dreamed. We built something real. Suddenly, my fear wasn't about surviving. It was about respect for him, for our seven kids combined. For the life we were building. If I could keep it together on my own for decades, I sure as hell could do it now, but this time with intention.

The truth is that being a badass isn't just about surviving divorce, death, or scarcity. It's about leaving behind clarity, not chaos.

And legacy isn't money. It's clean instructions, real love, and no mystery. So yeah, *that's* what made me deal with it.

Not one thing. All of it.

Why I put off prepping my will, and how I came to terms with it.

The part of the process that I put off the longest was the will. It's not that I didn't care or that I didn't understand the importance of the document. I did. I *do*.

But somewhere deep in my gut, I was terrified that if I wrote it down, if I dared to spell out what would happen if I died, I'd be inviting it. Tempting fate. Daring the universe to call my bluff.

It sounds irrational, but I'd already faced several near misses in my life. I'd been diagnosed with cancer in my late 20s and experienced a few other scares into my 40s (as mentioned, I'd lived through the grief of losing my stepmom and grandmother just days apart while eight months pregnant).

So, this mindset didn't feel irrational. It felt protective, as if I just *didn't say death's name out loud*, maybe it wouldn't come for me. I've always been the strong one. The saver. The hustler. The over-functioner.

And yet? My organization system is a beautiful dumpster fire.

I keep seven years' worth of taxes and home repair receipts in a plastic tote that also holds old birthday cards, some of the kids' crayon art, and God knows what else. The passports are in another box across the house with the birth certificates and Social Security cards. They're nestled somewhere between old flight itineraries, expired coupons, and ancient receipts of things I probably meant to return long ago.

It's a mess.

I know it's a mess.

But it's *my* mess. And for years I told myself it was fine because at least it was all kind of together in the same place, generally.

But the will was a different story. That wasn't just about finding important papers, it was about facing the unimaginable. It was about saying the quiet thing out loud: someday, I won't be here. And someone I love will be left trying to untangle my shit while also trying to breathe through the grief.

I couldn't stand the thought that my kids or my partner, this man I built a second-chance life with, would be left in the dark, unsure of what I wanted. Or worse, stuck cleaning up a mess I was too afraid to handle. The thing that finally made me get it done was love: big, inconvenient, grown-up love.

For my boys. For my man. For this full, chaotic life we'd pieced together.

In the end, we all sat down and did the thing as a team, side by side, sorting through the hard stuff and making the calls no one *wants* to make. Somewhere, in the middle of all that discomfort, the process stopped being about death and started being about care. About clarity, about making sure the people I love most never have to guess.

It's not perfect. It's not pretty. But it's *done*. And there's a sense of peace I didn't know I needed.

Real Girls Truth Bombs About Money, Wills, and All That Shit

Real Talk: Grown-ass women deserve more than vague advice and a haunted file drawer, take these timeless truths to heart as you're digging into all that scary-but-necessary paperwork.

1. *"You do not rise to the level of your goals. You fall to the level of your systems."*

—JAMES CLEAR, Author of *Atomic Habits*

2. *"A will isn't about dying. It's about protecting the people you love from drowning."*

—ANGELA BURK, Blogger and Author of *Real Girls Guide to Midlife*

3. *"We don't talk about money because we were taught it was tacky. But silence is expensive."*

—TIFFANY ALICHE, aka "The Budgetnista"

4. *"Your paycheck is not your worth. But your financial plan? That's your power."*

—SALLIE KRAWCHECK, Founder and Former CEO of Ellevest

5. *"Being prepared doesn't mean you're expecting to die. It means you love people enough not to leave them a mess."*

—CHANEL REYNOLDS, Author of *What Matters Most*

Bonus tip: Make a "Grab This First" folder and tell your people where the hell it is. Label it clearly. Include your will, medical directive, account info and logins, and a note that says: "If you're reading this, I love you. Now handle shit like a badass."

How to brace yourself for end-of-life prep that packs a punch.

What surprised me most when I started writing my will wasn't the logistics. It was the lump in my throat, the full-body flinch I didn't see coming. It was fear—pure, primal, and louder than I expected. Remember those two women I loved deeply, my grandma and my stepmom, who died two days apart? They'd been walking the same path facing terminal cancer. But their exits were night-and-day different.

My stepmom's passing had been peaceful. She let out a final, steady breath, and then there was stillness. She was ready. She was certain about her life, her legacy, where she was going, and how we'd all be OK.

But my grandma's death still haunts me. She was terrified. She gasped and struggled as if choking on the very thing she feared most, leaving us. Her whole life had been wrapped around her family. And in those final days, it felt like she couldn't find the air without us.

I always thought I'd be brave like them. But when it was my turn to plan and to write it all down, I came undone. I wasn't steady. I wasn't calm. Once again, I was cracked wide open by the realization that I wasn't ready to leave this life. I wasn't ready to part with my boys, my partner, or this messy, beautiful chaos we'd built. I put off end-of-life planning not because I didn't care but because I cared so much.

But then came the deeper truth:

They deserve peace more than I deserve to avoid fear. They deserve clarity, not a scavenger hunt through old paperwork and unanswered questions. They deserve a map, not a mess.

So, I sat in the discomfort. I did the work. I made the calls, chose the people and named the hard truths.

Clearing The Head Trash: Expert Q&A with Dr. Noah St. John

Meet Dr. Noah St. John—Author, Mindset Coach, and self-proclaimed "mental chiropractor." He's helped thousands of people rewrite their inner scripts and reclaim self-worth, wealth, and well-being. We asked him to break down the sneaky stories midlife women tell themselves about money, identity, and "starting over."

Q: You talk about "head trash"—how does that show up specifically around money and self-worth in midlife, especially for women who've spent decades prioritizing everyone else?

A: *Head trash is the voice in your head that says, "I'm not enough" or "I can't do it." For women in midlife who've spent years tending to everyone else—raising kids, supporting partners, managing lives— it can show up as guilt for investing in themselves, shame about not* being "further along," or fear that it's too late to build something new. They've been taught their worth comes from what they give, not what they create. Rewriting that belief is the first step to reclaiming financial and personal power.

Q: What advice do you give women who feel "behind" financially—not just in retirement savings, but in confidence and clarity?

A: *First, you're not behind—you're exactly where your experiences brought you. That "falling behind" feeling is rooted in shame and comparison. The antidote? One small win. Meet with a financial planner. Read a book that reframes your money mindset. Take one bold action. Confidence isn't a trait—it's a result of movement. Start where you are and build from there.*

Q: How can facing things like estate planning, wills, and long-term care be less about fear and more about power— especially after divorce, loss, or major life transitions?

A: *These decisions feel scary because they force us to confront endings. But really, they're about ownership—of your future, your choices, your legacy. After a major life shift, handling these things becomes one of the most radical acts of self-leadership. First step? Clear the head trash that says you're selfish or unprepared. You're not. You're ready.*

Q: Grieving who we used to be—physically, financially, emotionally—is real in midlife. What practices help women move through that without collapsing into shame or scarcity?

A: *Start with compassion. Midlife grief is often invisible—no one talks about mourning your younger body, your old dreams, or the years that slipped by. Honor that grief. Journal, get quiet, or join a group where it's safe to feel it. Then ask: "What do I want to create next?" You are not your past. You're the author of your next chapter.*

(continued)

Q: You call midlife an inflection point. What's one mindset shift every woman should make if she wants to rewrite her story—and her bank account?
A: *You're not starting over. You're starting now—with more wisdom, grit, and lived experience than ever before. This isn't a decline, it's a decision point. Stop shrinking. Claim your wealth, your voice, your space. Your value never came from your age, body, or relationship status. It comes from who you are—and it's time the world caught up.*

Tell them what you want, even in death.

The most powerful conversation I've ever had about my end-of-life wishes wasn't just about death—it was about *love.* The kind you build, the kind you leave behind, and the kind that shows up when shit gets real.

I told my boys clearly, with no hemming or hawing, that when I go, there's not going to be a funeral.

I want a party. Loud music. Full bar. And yes, my three sons are *required* to lead the dance floor accompanied by the euro disco vibes of ABBA's "Dancing Queen." That's non-negotiable. I want joy in the room, not just grief. I want them to laugh through the tears and feel me in every beat.

We talked about life-saving measures, too. About cremation. About not clinging if there's no quality of life left. Those were hard words to say out loud, but they mattered. What mattered even more was talking to my Aussie Man—the man I built this messy, beautiful second-chance life with—and telling him what I needed *from him* if I'm not here.

I needed to know he'd show up for my boys. That even from across the world, he'd be their soft place. Their steady hand. Their reminder that love doesn't vanish with loss, it just shifts shape.

I needed him to help them remember the life we built. Not perfectly, but honestly. With grit, laughter, forgiveness, and some knock-down-drag-out growth.

That conversation made me let go of the illusion that I could control everything. It taught me that *trust* is sometimes the deepest kind of love. I could hand it all over—my boys, my wishes, my hope for their future—and know that I'd chosen someone worthy of holding it all.

Because real love, the kind you fight for, bleed for, *build* with someone, is the kind of love that outlives you.

Expert Q&A with Nikoo N. Berenji: Partner at Berenji & Associates Family Law Attorneys, and Adjunct Law Professor at UCLA and USC

Nikoo Berenji brings more than a decade of experience representing hundreds of large corporations and individual defendants in a wide range of high-stakes legal matters. She's passionate about helping her clients access and obtain justice through the legal system, and she applies that passion to each and every family law matter she handles. She has appeared as a guest speaker on numerous legal topics, and is actively involved in numerous local non-profit boards and organizations. Nikoo is married and has two daughters. Here's her perspective on financial dos and don'ts in midlife:

Q: What's the biggest financial mistake women in midlife make when preparing for divorce, or avoiding it?
A: *One of the most common mistakes I see among our female clients who come to us seeking a divorce in midlife is avoidance. And that could be avoiding the divorce itself because the thought of having to deal with the financial (and emotional) fallout is overwhelming. Or it could look like avoiding understanding their financial situation and the details that will matter during the divorce process because it seems overwhelming and they often don't know where to start.*

Too many trust that their spouse will "do the right thing" and approach the process fairly. So, they don't take the time to truly figure out what's theirs, what they're entitled to, or how to begin protecting themselves. We see so many cases when reaching out to an attorney a little earlier, and/or some basic steps in advance of filing for divorce, would have resulted in these clients getting significantly more at the end of the case. But I think so many women in midlife have spent decades putting others ahead of themselves, and they hope that those sacrifices and all their effort will automatically count for something during court proceedings. Unfortunately, those assumptions—without adequate preparation and an understanding of the household finances—can leave them extremely vulnerable.

Bonus Tip: *If there's one thing I wish every woman had in place before walking into my office, it would be a clear picture of her own, and the family's, finances. Even if it's not totally accurate, a clear and honest list of what she owns, what the family owns, what they owe, what she and her spouse earn, and what they spend. Ideally, there would be documents verifying this information, such as tax returns, bank statements, property records and deeds, etc. Having that frame-work helps us hit the ground running, and makes it less likely that she'll miss out on money or assets to which she'd otherwise be entitled.*

Q: In your experience, how do power dynamics shift when a woman becomes financially independent in midlife, especially if she's been in a long-term marriage?
A: *This is one of the most rewarding shifts we see as family law attorneys, and it's not just about having more control over money. Especially in cases where our clients have spent years depending on someone else financially and putting their own needs last, new financial independence changes the emotional dynamic entirely. Many have convinced themselves that their needs or wants didn't matter or couldn't/shouldn't be prioritized because it wouldn't be "fair" because their spouse is the one who works outside of the home, or they weren't responsible for any of the family financial decisions. As if their own contributions to the family didn't matter as much.*

I've had clients tell me they didn't even realize how much they'd shrunk themselves in their marriages until they started having to make their own financial decisions—opening their own accounts, meeting with advisors, budgeting for their future. That shift can create a lot of confidence. And with confidence they suddenly see more options. Not just more options as far as how funds could be spent or what they could do, but even as far as staying in their marriage and maintaining the family status quo. We see lots of cases where women might start the divorce process with a lot of guilt and doubt about whether they're making the right choice. But once they start developing an understanding of the finances and become financially independent, that doubt fades away and they start to finally see leaving an unhappy marriage as a plausible option.

They often start asking for what they want in all areas of their lives more clearly (e.g. custody rights, demands about the course of the legal proceedings, and the case itself). We see them setting firmer boundaries in general, and a refusal to just accept what they're told. Sometimes that leads to conflict, but often it leads to clarity and confidence that they bring to all future decisions.

Q: What are the most overlooked legal documents every woman in midlife should have—whether she's married, divorced, single, or partnered?

A: *I think at the very least every woman in midlife should have a will, a power of attorney, and an advance healthcare directive. These are the basics—but they're often neglected, especially by women who don't see themselves as financially responsible for their family's well-being. A trust can be incredibly valuable, too, depending on what you own and what your goals are.*

Beyond the documents themselves, we also see women who overlook making sure the documents reflect their actual wishes. I've seen women forget to update their beneficiary designations after the divorce. That means that an ex-spouse can make claims to a retirement account or that a life insurance policy could accidentally go to an ex-spouse. Updating that one line on a form can make all the difference.

Q: You work with women who've spent decades putting everyone else first. What advice do you give to clients struggling with guilt, shame, or fear about claiming what's legally and rightfully theirs?

A: *First, I tell them they're not alone. The guilt is incredibly common— especially for women who've built their identities around caregiving, emotional labor, or being the "strong one" in the family, even for women who haven't been in that traditional role. My own mother was a perfect example of the latter—one of the most driven, financially independent women I know. But it took her years to make up her mind to file for divorce, because for so long she was worried how she'd be judged in our community, that she'd be harming my siblings and I, she even felt guilty about leaving my father alone! My brother and I often now talk about how we wish she would have done it sooner... we think it would have been better for us for a number of reasons. I often share this personal background with our clients who are struggling with guilt, shame and fear, from the perspective of the child they might be worried about hurting, even as someone who's seen how her own parents both came out of the process better off. Claiming what's yours isn't selfish, it's survival.*

The second thing I make sure I try to communicate is that they should set aside their guilt and shame precisely because of how much they care about those around them and their desire to put others first. I often use the oxygen mask on the plane analogy. If you're not financially secure, you can't help your kids, you can't support aging parents, and you can't rebuild your life in a healthy, empowered way. And modeling that kind of strength for your children, especially daughters, can be one of the most loving legacies you leave. You're not taking from anyone. You're stepping into what the law already recognizes as yours. And that shift, from shame to self-advocacy, is one of the most important parts of the process.

Q: How do you see estate planning as an act of emotional power, not just a financial one?

A: *I think estate planning is absolutely an act of emotional power. I didn't think that before I personally had my will and trust documents prepared years ago. The process forces you to really think about what your legacy will be, and what you want to leave behind. It's not just about dividing assets or naming beneficiaries. It's about declaring, "This is what matters to me. These are the people I want to protect. This is how I want to be remembered." Especially for women who've spent much of their lives being spoken over, the act of estate planning really can be profoundly empowering. You get to make decisions on your own terms. You get to prioritize the people and causes you care about most. It's not a process we often think of as "empowering" but I think it very much is. At a minimum it allows a woman to leave behind a message that says, "I mattered. I had a voice, and I used it."*

A quick note to the woman who handles everything, except her own death plan.

Dear Brilliant, Battle-worn, Soul-searching Woman in Midlife,

You are hereby granted full permission to stop treating your will like it's a cosmic jinx.

You're not summoning death. You're declaring: I love too hard to leave a mess.

That's not morbid. That's sacred.

This isn't about control. It's about care. For them and for you.

No, it's not fun. It's not sexy. But neither was surviving that breakup, that diagnosis, that death, that season where you held everyone else together while quietly falling apart.

You've already done the hard shit.

This? This is clarity.

Maybe you don't have a partner to hand it off to.

Maybe the family you'd otherwise count on is fractured, distant or just plain gone.

Maybe you're walking into uncharted territory, aging solo, grieving what never came, facing down transitions that feel too big to name.

That doesn't make you less worthy of peace. It makes you the reason this work matters.

Because even if no one's showing up for you the way you've shown up for others, you get to show up for yourself. That's legacy, too.

Remember these guiding principles as you're getting started:

- *Money was never just money. It was safety. Your end-of-life planning provides the same.*
- *Scarcity protected you. Now clarity can, too.*
- *You're allowed to want things to be easier for the people who love you and for the you that comes next.*

- *Even if no one's depending on you, you still get to own your ending.*

So, light a candle. Play some Nina Simone. Put your wishes in writing. Add ABBA's "Dancing Queen" if you want your ashes tossed with a side of glitter and sequins.

You don't owe the world your silence.

You don't owe your past a damn thing.

What you do owe yourself is this: They deserve peace even if "they" is just you.

And you deserve to walk toward it unafraid.

Sincerely, Angela
(your sister in loss, reinvention and that "I'll deal with it later" energy)

CHAPTER 12

What If My Body Doesn't Bounce Back?

For a long while I'd say I had a pretty easy ride with the whole aging-body thing. Pregnancy didn't wreck me. My joints held steady. In my mind I chalked it up to exercise (running aka "therapy in motion"), decent eating habits, and a healthy dose of smug, long-lived Norwegian DNA strands swimming in my gene pool.

But somewhere between Baby No. 1 and perimenopause, my body sent out the first tiny distress signal: let's call it The Boob Situation.

We went from perky B-cups to sad little prunes practically overnight. They didn't just deflate, they surrendered. Like, "*Ma'am, we did our job and we're retiring.*" That was the first real shapeshifter. But I still bounced back. Kinda. Or at least I convinced myself I did.

Then came the slow creep. The knees complaining going up (or down) stairs. The hands aching while opening a pickle jar. Somehow my eyelids folded themselves into tiny tents of defeat. My face looked tired. And if you've ever had someone say, "You look tired," especially when it's your man's ex and she means '*You look old as shit*,' you know that kind of comment sticks to your soul like melted gum on a hot sidewalk.

The real kicker came while running in shorts one summer in my early

50s. I glanced down at my thighs and saw what I can only describe as *haunted tissue paper flapping in the breeze.*

Runners: Do NOT look at your legs mid-stride after 50. You will not recover.

Then came the bizarre WTF changes: thinning hair, a soft belly, wild weight swings, and a neck that had clearly thrown in the towel.

And here's another thing I didn't see coming (but apparently should have braced for): nose growth. A friend in her early 60s pulled me aside and said, "Did anyone warn you that your nose keeps growing?" Um, no, ma'am, they did not. But now I can't unsee it—on her, on others, and probably someday, on me.

As for the metabolism? It had fully broken up with me. In my 40s, if I wanted to drop five pounds, I could skip a bagel, take a few brisk walks, and boom, back in my favorite jeans. In my 50s? Forget it. I can drink water and gain weight. My body's like, *"Cute try, we're in storage mode now."*

My face now features jowls that look like I'm storing emotional baggage in my cheeks. The old curves? Gone. They packed up and made room for new bumps, weird ripples, and those sneaky little shifts that whisper: *You're not who you were, but look at you, still standing, wink, wink.*

And then there are the scars.

One on my neck from cancer. One on my leg from a cancerous tumor found and removed during COVID-19. The horizontal C-section line that delivered two boys into the world. Still another from a rogue growth that appeared after Baby No. 3. My body, it turns out, is a bit of a botanical garden for tumors.

Even my childhood scar, the one on my chin from when I was four has changed shape and color. Like it's aging with me, like it knows somehow.

These weren't "bounce back" moments. They were reminders. Soft but firm: *You pushed hard. You survived. But did you ever stop and care for yourself the way you cared for everyone else?*

No, the changes weren't all dramatic, they didn't hit like a wrecking ball, but they *etched*. Each one quietly reshaped how I see myself, what I've carried, ignored, and overcome. They forced me to admit how long I've gone without praising this body. Without thanking her.

Now, finally, I'm starting to give her the respect she's earned.

My Body Isn't "Bouncing Back," She's Becoming

Midlife isn't about "getting your body back." It's about getting your *self* back. Because what if the bounce-back isn't the goal? What if it's the burn-down that sets you free? "Midlife isn't about fighting change," says Jacqui Burge, Wellness Coach and Founder of XO Jacqui, "It's about building a sustainable foundation of wellness that evolves with you."

Jacqui's right. Your body's not betraying you, it's telling the truth. About stress. About sugar. About pushing too hard for too long. Cortisol will spike, cravings will hit harder, and your old coping tools will stop working. This isn't failure. This is the body saying: the old way doesn't fit anymore. And in that unraveling? There's power.

At Goddess Retreats in Bali, Founder and Surf Instructor Chelsea Ross has watched women in their 50s and 60s reclaim adventure, courage, and the physical joy they were once told was behind them. "They aren't surfing to prove anything," she says. "They're doing it because they finally gave themselves permission to try. It's not anti-aging, it's staying youthful as a way of being."

Still struggling with physical grief? You're not alone. Kimberly Sheridan, PhD, Midlife Mother and Author who navigated caregiving, empty nesting and reinvention all at once, says the turning point was asking: "'What am I still holding that's no longer mine?' Anyone rooted in the past needs a new vision for the future. That's the only way to release what was."

And if you're staring at your face on Zoom all day wondering who that woman is, Diane Lang, Counselor, Coach and Author of *Mindfully Happy: Waking Up to Life*, gets it. The constant up-close exposure, and the filtered, flawless social scroll that follows, messes with our minds. "We start to compare ourselves to filtered versions of everyone else," she says. "And then we look in the mirror and feel even more disappointed. But filters aren't real, you are."

Traci Griffin, Founder of Achieve Greatness Daily, knows this too well. After surviving breast cancer and being laid off just two weeks post-surgery, she found herself grieving more than just her body—she was facing the collapse of identity, stability, and everything she'd worked for. But it sparked something new: "I wasn't chasing a role anymore. I was building something real."

She took the exact tools that helped her survive the spiral and turned them into the THRIVE Method—a six-part framework for helping women rebuild after loss, illness or burnout. "Reinvention isn't about starting over," says Traci, "It's about living in alignment with who you've become."

Missy Toy Ozeas, the energy healer, sees it from the inside out. Her clients carry grief, resentment, and self-abandonment in their cells. But it's not woo, it's truth. When women stop pushing and start listening, their healing begins. "What if your body isn't asking for more effort, but for permission to let go," she says.

And then there's the deeper shift, less visible, more vital. Nicky Price, Transformation Therapist and Success Coach, sees it all the time: midlife women who've hit every benchmark—career, caregiving, marriage, motherhood—yet still feel like they've disappeared inside their own lives. "Midlife is often less about physical aging and more about emotional awakening," she says.

Nicky works with women who are finally asking: '*Is this it? Where did I go? Do I still matter?*' The truth? They're not broken, they're becoming. It's not just hormones or hot flashes, it's the unraveling of identities shaped by decades of over giving and self-silencing. "Skincare, nutrition, and hormone support are all valuable, but so is the identity shift," Nicky says. "This is about reconnecting to your purpose, your voice, your confidence."

Yes, the brain fog and sleep disruption are real. But so is the quiet, fierce opportunity to re-meet yourself. To become visible. To take up space. To finally say, *I matter*. Nicky helps women uncover the patterns that no longer serve them, so they can rewrite their story with agency, power, and purpose. Because this isn't about returning to who you were, it's about rising into who you're here to be. You are not a before-and-after photo. You are becoming. And she is no longer asking for permission.

Here's what we're done with:

- "Just lose the weight and you'll feel better" advice.
- Bounce-back culture that ignores what it costs.
- Shame for slowing down, speaking up, or saying no.

Here's what we're claiming:

- Joy over judgment.
- Strength over size.
- Curiosity over comparison.

Doctors can dismiss you, but they can't defeat you.

What about self-respect? In midlife we often have to deliver the goods themselves, because the medical establishment won't always be ready with a trophy.

Case in point: I recently walked into my longtime OB/GYN's office, a practice I've been with for twenty-five fucking years. I had braced myself to talk about some pretty intimate and bewildering stuff. The kind of stuff you *hope* a trusted provider will meet with curiosity and actual medical expertise. Not blank stares and polite nods.

I came armed with a laundry list of symptoms: specifically, a pee problem that blindsided me, and libido changes that felt like someone had flipped the off switch without asking. I also wanted to know why the hell, years after my period stopped at 47, my body was suddenly serving up new symptoms like it was trying to win some kind of hormonal chaos award.

I asked about bloodwork. Thyroid levels. A bladder ultrasound, especially given my history of a tumor that grew *between* my uterus and bladder after Baby No. 3. And let's not forget we never got clean margins on that sucker.

Her response? A few long sighs. Some "*I know, it's hard*" sympathy. And a whole lot of *nothing*.

Oh, and she whisper-talks. WHISPERS.

Did I mention I have hearing loss that I've been ignoring for far too long? (Yes, I'm dealing with it now thanks to the terrifying hearing-loss-as-a-prelude-to-dementia stats dropped on me by my partner's daughter and her wife, both nurses, both badasses). But imagine sitting there, raw and vulnerable, and *you can't even hear the brush-off you're getting*. That's next-level disrespect.

I walked out of that office shaking with rage. Not just for me, but for *all of us*.

Then I had dinner with a friend who sees the *same* doctor. She shared her own horror story: an IUD removal turned surgical, a list of unanswered questions about what it meant in her mid-50s, and the same sympathetic nods. That nod? It's the new middle finger of women's healthcare.

Here's what I've learned: You have to fight. You have to research. You have to ask the hard questions and be willing to walk out, start over, and say "no more." Even to doctors you've known for decades. ESPECIALLY to them.

Because if this is how we're treated with relatively "simple" concerns, what happens to the woman whose symptoms are complex, or scary, or don't fit neatly into the little menopause pamphlet?

This isn't just about bad bedside manner. This is about women being dismissed, diminished, and denied the care we *deserve*. We are not too complicated. We are not "just aging."

And we sure as hell aren't here for the nod-and-sigh treatment. Not anymore.

The midlife maintenance plan (with science, sass and a splash of woo-woo).

Real Talk: I've found that women approach midlife wellness in different ways. It's one of the many things that makes us awesome.

Some women meditate. Me? I schedule my OB/GYN, endo, dentist, and urologist appointments like I'm trying to win a chronic-condition bingo card. It might not be sexy, but it's sacred. I've got a full rotation of seven providers and honestly need a project manager just to keep the appointment reminders straight.

And yes, flossing counts—when I remember to do it. (Twice a week, if I'm feeling spiritually aligned. Sue me.)

Running is my sanity, always has been. It's not about burning calories. It's about the *me time*. I can be pissed off, spaced out, hormonal, or just trying to outrun whatever *Real Housewife* drama I've got playing in my earbuds (Bravo TV is my religion). I'm not someone's mom, partner, or employee in those miles. That time is all *mine*.

Meanwhile, some of us are operating a full-blown pharmacy out of our bathroom drawer: turmeric, glucosamine, ginkgo, powdered greens, mysterious mushroom blends that promise cellular rebirth. And collagen? It's practically become its own food group.

Some of it works. Some of it is peer pressure in capsule form. But we're trying it all because NO ONE TOLD US ANYTHING!

And midlife doesn't come with a syllabus.

We've got women on HRT, others microdosing mushrooms, and more still living off protein shakes that taste like sadness. Some have red-light masks and La Mer. Others scream into the void while stabbing a jade roller into their under-eye bags. We're out here doing pelvic floor therapy trying to keep our insides *inside*, performing glute bridges to offset a butt that's trying to relocate to our thighs, and practicing gentle stretching for joints that now pop like bubble wrap.

We try things. We share the wins. We ditch what flops.

Because we do not gatekeep. We don't keep secrets. We share what works, what's bullshit, and what helped us feel even *slightly* less like we're unraveling in the vitamin aisle at CVS.

The most radical act of love, though? Giving a shit about your body, your brain, your rest, your boundaries, and your weird little rituals. Moisturizing like your face owes you money. Booking the bloodwork. Doing the Kegels. Saying no when your soul says, "Hell, no." And telling younger women the truth: aging is a gift. It just shows up wrapped in saggy skin, hot flashes, and the occasional audible knee pop.

Midlife wellness isn't one-size-fits-all. But the more we talk about it, the less alone we all feel.

Grief, Aging and Finding Your Way Back to You: Real Talk with Aging Expert Diane Lang, M.A.

Diane Lang is a Counselor, Coach, and Speaker with 25+ years of experience in psychology, positive aging, and resilience. She's taught college-level psych, worked with TBI patients, and just released her fourth book on happiness and whole-person well-ness, titled *Mindfully Happy: Waking Up to Life.* But what makes Diane different? She doesn't just talk about aging from the neck down—she talks about the emotional journey no one preps us for.

Here's Diane on:

Q: Why the mirror messes with us.

A: *The "Zoom effect" is real.* "We're staring at our own faces con-stantly—on calls, in selfies, everywhere—and we start spotting every little thing we don't like," *says Diane. She sees clients compare themselves to their parents (and not in a loving way), or stare into the mirror feeling like strangers in their own skin. Her fix? Exposure therapy with a twist.* "Look at yourself in the mirror for five to ten minutes daily—but shift the focus. What's working? What's beautiful? What's yours to love?" *She adds:* "The women I envied in my 30s? They were in their 50s. They were wiser. Kinder to themselves. And gave way fewer shits."

Q: Grieving who you were—and still loving who you are.

A: *Grieving isn't just for death and divorce.* "We have to grieve the life we thought we'd have," *says Diane.* "Maybe the career didn't work out, or the kids left and you're wondering what's next. That identity confusion is real." *But grief isn't the enemy—resistance is.* "Real acceptance means sitting with the hard stuff, naming the loss, and making decisions from clarity—not fear. That's where reinvention starts," *she says.*

(continued)

Q: The pressure to 'bounce back.'
A: *Whether it's after menopause, illness, or life blowing up, the bounce-back myth needs a rewrite. "It's not about snapping back," Diane says. "It's about reflecting on what happened, noticing patterns, asking what it taught you—and then shifting forward. Resilience isn't born, it's built." Her tip: Write about the hardest thing you've survived. Then ask, What did I learn? What did I need to get through it? You'll remember how strong you are.*

Q: Aging "wrong" and letting go of the comparison game.
A: *"There's no such thing as aging wrong," Diane says flatly. "We're all writing our own story." Still clinging to outdated beliefs, like retirement by 55 or fading into invisibility post-menopause? Time to rewrite the script. "Ask yourself: Where did that belief come from? Is it mine, or something I inherited?" she says. Her advice: Define what aging means to you—then live that truth out loud.*

Love her, grieve her, become her: How to honor what's changed and still feel like a queen.

My quietest grief? Thinking I could control it all.

That if I ran far enough, ate clean enough, stayed strong enough, I'd somehow get a pass on the wear and tear. That if I just did everything right, I could hold the line on gravity, hormones, exhaustion, and the creeping *"WTF is happening to me?"* symptoms no one warned us about.

Midlife, however, said: Hold my wine.

The sexiness? Some days it packs a bag and disappears. The pee problem is demoralizing, and nothing says "humbling" like throwing out your back picking up a T-shirt. I now take a full five seconds to stand up straight.

Five. Seconds.

My joints snap like gravel in a blender, and that's just the walk to the kitchen. My neck's making sounds I can only describe as haunted.

My boobs? We've had an entire story arc: perky, powerful, used, deflated, resurrected, and now, in their droopier encore years, still down to party. They've fed babies, sparked insecurity, drawn comments (some adorable, some devastating), and now, become something I've reclaimed. For me.

I've lost strength. I've lost shape. I've lost pieces of myself I didn't even realize were sacred until they were gone, until I saw my body in the mirror and thought, '*Oh. You've been through it, haven't you?*' She has. And I never thanked her for it.

I grieve not taking care of her sooner. I grieve all the years I ignored her, minimized her, let other people's words define her. The high school crush who said my lips were too big and my butt too flat. The ex who made "observations" that stuck like needles in my psyche. The years I believed those throwaway lines were truth.

But here's what's also true: This body is a fucking miracle.

She gave birth to three wild boys. She showed up to the mediator's office and held it together during my divorce. She flew 8000 miles to love again. She danced in kitchens, yelled from the sidelines, and carried me across finish lines. She was the jungle gym, the life raft, the pillow, and the safety net for my kids.

She got me through cancer, twice. And now? She gets complimented at the beach. Not because she's perfect, but because she's powerful. And she knows it.

I have a butt now, by the way. Or maybe I always did and I finally stopped letting some adolescent moron tell me otherwise. My lips? Still big, still luscious, and still saving me thousands in filler. And my smile? It's crooked, bold, and takes over my whole face. I love it now. Because I said so.

The fierce joy is in the knowing.

Knowing I can walk into a room and feel beautiful, not for how I look, but for who I am. Knowing I don't need to be "sexy" to be desired. Knowing I can show up in denim and lashes, or sweatpants and puffy eyes, and still be worthy of being seen. Knowing that wellness in midlife isn't about perfection, it's about maintenance, grace, pelvic-floor therapy, supplements that might be total bullshit, and doing whatever the hell it takes to feel like you again.

The freedom is in the reclaiming.

I don't owe anyone an explanation for the Botox, the boobs, the workouts, the naps or the boundaries. I don't owe youth to anyone. And I sure as hell don't owe silence. This body? She's been my ride-or-die. And now, finally, I show up for her, too.

We're not just aging. We're evolving. With a few extra stretch marks, some creaks in our joints, and one seriously powerful "Fuck you" to the myths we were sold about what we lose in midlife.

Turns out, we gain more than we ever expected when we finally stop apologizing for the skin we're in.

Expert Wisdom Worth Holding Onto

Real Talk: Midlife is less about what we lose and more about what we reclaim. Here's several timeless truths to embrace, even when your body isn't having it:

1. *"Pelvic floor therapy should be as normal as dental cleaning. Even if you haven't had kids, this matters for bladder control, painfree sex, and mobility."*

—DR. ANNE DUCH, Women's Health Physical Therapist

2. *"Stop trying to fix your body. It was never broken."*

—V, formerly Eve Ensler, Playwright of *The Vagina Monologues*

3. *"I had to learn to love the body that had kept score. The one that had carried me through it all. That was my revolution."*

—SONYA RENEE TAYLOR, Author of *The Body Is Not an Apology*

4. *"I do what I do… On a morning run, I realized… 'Remember her? She's still in there somewhere. Why don't you go get her?' That lit a pilot light in my tummy."*

—DAVINA MCCALL, TV Presenter & Midlife Wellness Advocate

5. *"Your body is the home you will live in the longest. Make peace with her. Give her grace. She's earned it."*

—DR. THEMA BRYANT, Psychologist & Best Selling Author

Another love letter to my aging body: Don't give up.

Dear Younger Me,

OK sweetheart, lean in. I've got some things to whisper in your ear that you won't find in a Cosmo quiz or on your mom's nightstand.

First: Moisturize your neck. I'm serious. Start now.

Second: Your body isn't a project. She's not here to be fixed, shrunk, or constantly apologized for. She's your ride-or-die. So, stop calling her names and start saying thank you.

Third: Yes, your boobs will one day resemble sad little prunes. They will retire early. They will not ask permission. But don't worry, you'll figure it out. And you'll eventually love them again, even when they're droopy, lopsided, or being lovingly enjoyed by someone who knows exactly how lucky they are.

Fourth: You'll throw your back out picking up a sock. You'll get winded by stairs that once flirted with you. You'll look in the mirror one day and see your grandmother blinking back, crow's feet, soft chin, wavy skin and all. And instead of panicking, you'll smile. Because she's always been beautiful.

And now? So are you.

Also, thongs. Let's talk about them. You'll break up with them in your 40s and feel wildly liberated. Then, in your mid 50s, you'll get a wild hair and try one on again, only to realize Satan's shoelace is now sawing you in half. You'll rip that thing off with the rage of a woman who's had enough and sprint back into the soft, glorious arms of below-the-belly briefs. And yes, you'll even find yourself winking at the high-rise ones that flirt with your belly button. No shame. Just comfort, baby.

You'll carry babies, loss, rage, joy, stress, cancer, heartbreak and healing in this body. And she will still show up for you every day. Don't you dare take her for granted.

Also, fair warning: You will one day own an entire drawer of supplements, pee a little when you sneeze, and do Kegels in line at the grocery store. It's fine. No one can tell.

And finally: You won't be everyone's cup of tea (man, do I hate that tired old phrase), but fuck tea, unless it's one of your girlfriend's spilling it. You'll become your own top-shelf, smooth-but-dangerous shot of whiskey. The kind that burns a little going down and leaves a hell of an impression.

Keep going. She's not perfect, but she's battle-tested, wildly loyal, and completely unstoppable. And she's all yours.

With Love,

Your Older, Bolder, Badass Self

P.S. Toss the thong, she had a good run.

CHAPTER 13

Party of One and Proud of It (Or at Least Making Peace with It)

When I let myself sit in the imagined silence of this phase of life without a partner or kids, the first emotion that rises is fear.

Not a loud, screaming fear. It's the quieter kind. The kind that lingers in the corners of the room after everyone has gone home. The kind that creeps in after dark, when the TV is off, the laundry is folded, and there's no one asking what's for dinner. It's the fear of getting sick. The fear of not having someone there. The fear of feeling irrelevant.

And yet, I know this fear is not unique to me.

I'm a mom to three biological sons and four bonus kids. And even with all that love, there were still nights after my divorce when I sat in my room alone, too heartbroken to be in the family room that no longer felt like mine.

I worked. I parented. I checked the boxes. But at night, I disappeared. I hid. The stillness didn't feel like peace then. It felt like punishment. But over time, something shifted.

The quiet became a container for reflection. And if I listened closely, it started whispering truths I'd ignored for years.

Truth: I was scared, but I was also strong.

Truth: I missed the noise, but I needed the space.

Truth: I was never meant to disappear inside someone else's expectations of motherhood, womanhood, or partnership.

I've come to understand the weight of solitude not just from my own experience but from the women around me, friends who are child-free by choice or by circumstance. Women who have been made to feel like they must have "forgotten" to prioritize children, as if motherhood is the only proof of a life well-lived.

One friend told me how she endured years of scrutiny, the kind that's wrapped in *faux* concern but steeped in judgment.

"You'll regret it someday," they said. "It's not too late."

But what if it *is* late? What if it's exactly the right time to live out loud, unapologetically and define meaning on our own terms?

There is a fierce kind of freedom that lives inside solitude. It doesn't arrive on Day 1. It sneaks in slowly, disguised as small rituals: lighting a candle for no one but yourself, dancing in the kitchen with a glass of wine, booking a trip because you can. And, yes, sometimes crying into your soup because your grown kids don't need you the same way anymore—and neither does anyone else.

But then comes the knowing:

- The knowing that you can build your own blueprint for love and connection, whether that looks like co-housing, community dinners, or soulmates who come in the form of girlfriends with passports and beach bags.
- The knowing that relevance doesn't require a partner or a baby or a gold star.
- The knowing that while some of us are still waking up next to someone, and others are waking up alone, all of us *get to choose ourselves* at last.

For me, that choice came with a love story I never expected. It spans 8000 miles, more plane tickets than I can count, and the kind of emotional intimacy that only shows up when you stop performing and start being real. But this chapter isn't about whether you have a partner or not. It's about asking the harder question: Who are you when no one's watching?

The answer won't come easily. But I promise it's worth waiting for.

Feel the fear. Grieve the noise. Then rise anyway.

We always do.

Expert Q&A with Michelle Cantrell: LPCC, Couples Therapist, Midlife Reclaimer, and Romantic Realist

After her 28-year marriage ended, Michelle Cantrell didn't just survive, she rewired. As a licensed therapist and founder of The Center for Growth & Connection, she now helps women do the same: unpack shame, reimagine intimacy, and rediscover what it means to be loved without performance. Her story is both a mirror and a map for anyone staring down reinvention with a tender heart and a stretch-marked body.

Q: When your "forever" story ends after 28 years, what does day one of the "Now what?" chapter actually look like?
A: *Day one was brutal. I didn't bounce into empowerment—I curled up on the floor sobbing, heart pounding, wondering how the life I'd built for over three decades had just vanished. I had orbited my identity around my partner, and without that anchor, I was lost. Rewriting my definition of love took time, through therapy, walking my dogs alone, journaling, letting friends hold me. I had to unlearn the idea that love had to be earned and start asking: What does it feel like to be fully myself with someone?*

Q: What surprised you most about dating again after 50?

A: *That I liked it. In my marriage, I was always trying to be chosen. Now? I get to choose. I ask: Do I feel safe? Desired? Seen? Sure, there were cringe texts and awkward first kisses, but also deep joy, real chemistry, and the revelation that I don't need to shrink to be loved. I'm now with someone who is present, nurturing, attuned and fun. It's not perfect. It's better. It's true.*

Q: How have you helped women, and yourself, unpack shame around being "too needy, too late, or too complicated" for love?

A: *I believed all that, too. In my marriage I minimized my needs to keep the peace. It didn't make me easier to love—it just made me invisible. Now I teach women to reframe the narrative: your needs aren't too much—they're just unmet. I've never felt more sensual than I do now. Sex isn't about performance anymore, it's about presence and pleasure. And yes, it can still be electric. It might not be everyone's story, but I'm proof it's possible.*

Q: How does love shift when the goal isn't a white picket fence—it's truth, pleasure, and partnership without performance?

A: *It's liberating. I'm not auditioning for love anymore. I'm living it. The relationship I'm in now isn't built on anxiety or fantasy, it's built on truth. We laugh, we argue, we're bored sometimes, and it all counts. Love now means resonance: Do I feel alive? Safe? Real? That's the new fairytale.*

Q: What would you say to the woman staring at her empty bed, her stretch-marked thighs, and a heart that's been through it, wondering if love is still on the menu?

A: *Yes, love is still on the damn menu. So is sex. And Sunday pancakes with someone who touches your face like it's sacred. But it starts with you. Sleep in the middle of the bed. Take up space. Play your music loud. That heart? It's not broken, it's breaking open.*

Unpartnered, unbothered, unstoppable:
Solo and seriously thriving.

Let me start here: I have a friend who is, by every definition, brilliant, bold, and badass.

Her life is full and rich. She travels the world, pours herself into her work and friendships, and loves her family with everything she has. But when she was younger her choice not to have kids was met with ridicule. Not just passing comments but pointed cruelty. Women, men, work colleagues and her own family all scorned her choice.

Their insinuation was always the same: *You must've forgotten to prioritize family. You made an oversight. You committed a clerical error in the ledger of womanhood.*

As stated before, this too cracked me open.

Because: What the hell? How have we built a culture where a woman's agency is treated like a mistake?

Another story came to me through a friend's circle. A woman chose, in her mid-40s, to have a baby on her own. You'd think people would applaud the strength and clarity it takes to do that. Nope.

She caught hell. Not from strangers, but from the people closest to her. Judgment masquerading as concern. Condescension in the name of love. The people who should've thrown her a parade acted like she was irresponsible or naive. It gutted me.

I know foster moms who give so much of themselves, who carry the emotional weight of care without the traditional title of "mother."

I know women who've faced impossible decisions about adoption, about raising a sibling's child, about stepping in and stepping away when they knew they weren't equipped to do more.

Those decisions are brutal. And still, those women stood. With grief. With heartbreak. With the weight of it all. And I also know this: For some of us, the circle is getting smaller. Not in a bitter way, but in an intentional, unflinching one.

The older we get the more forks in the road appear. Sometimes that means realizing the friendships that once held us together are no longer aligned. I've seen women reconnect with old friends after years apart, only to discover that the glue is gone. Without the kids in the same grade, the Friday happy hours or the shared career grind, there's just not much left.

And it hurts.

Sometimes, we sit across from someone we once adored, coffee in hand, memories between us, and we realize the "there" is no longer there. Especially if you didn't have kids or they did. That common bond doesn't exist anymore. The energy is off. The values have shifted. And no one's wrong, but the friendship's gone. It's a quieter kind of grief. The mourning of old closeness. Of people who knew your inside jokes and your break-ups. But midlife makes you choosy. There's less time, less tolerance for performative connection.

In midlife, the brave thing isn't holding on. It's letting go.

What I feel under all these stories is one word: bravery. Not the glossy kind. Not the #bossbabe "you got this" kind. I'm talking real, gut-deep bravery. Bravery to face judgment. Bravery to live outside the script. Bravery to grieve what never was or what might've been. Bravery to stand anyway.

Have they faced hard emotions? Yes.

Turned away from friends or family who weren't safe? Yep.

Stared down the barrel of regret or sorrow? 100%.

Ten toes in the dirt, they have stood strong. And they keep standing.

Some of the fiercest, most vibrant women I know are child-free. By choice, by circumstance, by pain, by peace. They are aunties, sisters, friends, lovers, mentors, CEOs, surgeons, soldiers, nurses, artists. They are the most loyal humans I know.

And let's not forget those in same-sex partnerships who either couldn't or chose not to have kids. The courage it takes to exist in a society that often invalidates your relationship *and* your family structure, on top of the sanctimonious BS from your own family or random internet trolls? It's exhausting. And it's real.

What these women have taught me is that motherhood isn't the only legacy. That love isn't limited to blood. That the makeup of our family isn't predefined but instead is something we get to choose. That a woman who walks the solo path isn't broken—she is complete.

These stories gutted me because they showed me what real autonomy looks like, and what a truly full life can be. Even when it looks nothing like the brochure.

5 Experts on Designing a Future That's Yours Alone (Literally)

Real Talk: Here are five expert truths to include in your party-of-one manifesto. May they inspire fierce and intentional living in midlife.

1. *Define your values and befriend your fear.*

Life Coach Anna Olson argues that intentional solo aging starts with knowing what matters and confronting the what-ifs head on.

2. *Solo living isn't a health hazard. It can enable you to thrive.*

Aging experts report that "solo agers" live long, happy lives when they build support, plan ahead, and claim it as valid and vibrant.

3. *Child-free by choice or chance. Still bold. Still whole.*

Marcia Drut-Davis, trailblazing Author and Truth-Teller, has spent decades fighting the narrative that says women who don't have kids "forgot" or "settled." Be assured your choice is one full of meaning, not shame.

4. *Solo midlife isn't a pity party, it's a freedom zone.*

Maddy Dychtwald, Longevity Expert and Reinventioin Queen, calls midlife a "freedom zone." It's a time to lean into autonomy, health, and growth—sometimes for the first time in decades.

5. *You are the architect of your aging identity.*

Pasqualina Perrig-Chiello, Psychologist, Researcher and aging badass, shows that midlife transition can be harnessed as a powerful portal for self-crafted meaning, not a crisis to overcome.

Got opinions about my solo life?
Grab a seat, I've got stories and zero patience.

Oh girl, pour the wine. Leave the judgment at the door. Let's go...

If I could sit across from a brilliant, beautiful woman (maybe even you, dear reader) who'd been told she "must've forgotten to prioritize children," I'd look her dead in the eyes and say:

Are you fucking kidding me?

You didn't *forget*. You didn't misplace a baby on your way to a career or accidentally skip motherhood while you were out here living a full-ass life. You *chose*. Or maybe life chose for you. But either way, there was no forgetting.

What people are *really* uncomfortable with is a woman who owns her time, her body, her energy, and refuses to let someone else define her worth by her womb. And don't even get me started on the way society clutches its pearls when a woman dares to prioritize her *freedom*, her *peace* or, God forbid, her *pleasure* over raising children.

It's as if being child-free automatically makes you selfish, broken or somehow less evolved.

Newsflash: *Motherhood is not the only form of legacy.*

Nurturing. Protecting. Showing up. Creating joy. Building something from scratch. That shit takes many forms. And not one of them requires a diaper bag.

You've mothered ideas. You've mothered careers. You've mothered friends and siblings and causes. Hell, some of you have mothered your own mothers. The truth is, *mother* isn't a job title, it's a verb. It's a frequency. It's love in motion. And *you* have never stopped loving this world with every fierce, fearless, fuck-it-I'm-doing-it-my-way cell in your body.

So here is my toast to you:

- To the women who didn't forget a damn thing.
- To the women who refused the script and wrote their own.
- To the ones who are godmothers, mentors, aunties, truth-tellers, creators, and cycle-breakers.
- To all of you.

You didn't forget.

You remembered *you*. And that is the most radical thing a woman can do.

Solo Doesn't Mean Small, It Means Sovereign

Aging solo is not a tragedy. It's not a character flaw. It's not something you "forgot" to fix while everyone else was stockpiling husbands and family portraits. As Dr. Nivedita Nayak, Clinical Psychologist and midlife transition expert who you'll remember from Chapter 4, reminds us: The solo path is more common than anyone wants to admit.

Whether it's divorce, widowhood, a life outside motherhood, or a conscious choice to roll solo, more women than ever are aging without a traditional partner or kid-in-the-picture. And the cultural script? Still stuck in the 1950s. "I never thought I'd be doing this alone," says Christine, a woman in her 60s. "But, I'm also more free than I've ever been."

Can we talk about the grief *and* the glory?

Yes, there's grief. For the life you imagined. The milestones you watched everyone else hit. The weird silence on holidays when people don't quite know where to place you. That part is real. And it deserves naming. But here's the part nobody talks about: The power. The permission. The absolute radical agency of living a life that belongs to *you*, not your kids, not your ex, not your parents' blueprint.

Dr. Nayak captures it beautifully: "We need to reframe solitude. It's not lacking. It's clarity. You get to decide what's sacred now. Your energy. Your bed. Your joy. Your time. Your next act."

Chosen family > Default expectations

You don't have to live in a commune (although let's be honest, girl-group porch wine therapy is wildly underrated). But you *do* need to build support intentionally. Emotionally. Medically. Financially. Socially. That means:

- Creating a care network that doesn't rely on a spouse or adult child to manage your life.
- Making health plans while you're healthy, not in a crisis.
- Investing in friendships that don't guilt trip you for choosing yourself.

Because aging solo doesn't mean being *alone*. It means being *at choice*. "If I meet a man who compliments where I'm going—great. And if not, that's fine too," says Kimberly Sheridan, the PhD, Life Coach and Founder of Fueled By Soul who we last heard from in the previous chapter.

Space, guilt, and sacred solitude.

A recurring theme from the women I spoke to: craving private space and feeling guilty about it. We need to end that shame spiral right here. Wanting solitude isn't selfish, it's survival. Whether it's five minutes locked in the bathroom or a full week-end with no one asking you for shit, needing space is a sign you're alive and paying attention to your own needs. That is midlife wisdom, not weakness.

To all the ladies flying solo:
Single doesn't equal doomed.

Dear You,

Let's not sugarcoat this. The fear of dying alone? It's real. It's deep. It's primal. It's 3 a.m.-panic-attack-under-the-covers real. I've felt it. I've lived it.

Some nights, I spiraled so far into that fear that I couldn't tell if I was grieving a future that hadn't happened or mourning the fantasy I'd clung to for too long. You're not wrong for feeling it. Don' t let anyone tell you you're "not evolved" because you don't want to die in silence or sickness with no one in the next room.

You're not weak for admitting that even your fiercest independence gets heavy some days. That the silence isn't always peace, sometimes it's a punishment. But here's the other truth I had to claw my way to: Settling doesn't save you.

Shrinking to fit into someone else's box doesn't protect you. Performing "enough-ness" just to stave off aloneness can kill your soul long before the body ever gives out. There was a time I thought partnership was the only way to feel safe. That love—romantic love—was the armor. I've since learned that safety doesn't always come with a ring or a warm body next to you.

Sometimes, it's whispered by the women who hold your secrets and your spine in the middle of the night... The women who've seen your face swollen from crying and still pick you up at the airport in a caftan and lip gloss. The community you build, the rituals you honor, the hard boundaries you keep.

My circle now? They're not just my emergency contacts, they're my spiritual life-lines, my late-night truth-tellers, and the ones who call me on my own bullshit when I start spiraling or just plain get it wrong. They rage with me when life feels unfair, hold space when I'm unraveling, and remind me that while love isn't always tidy, it shouldn't shrink you.

And while I've got my steady, solid Aussie Man beside me now, the one who doesn't flinch when I show up messy or loud, I still check in with my girls. Because real love doesn't isolate you. It expands you. And any life worth living better make room for both the big love and the badass circle who helped you rebuild.

So, to you, my sister in this beautiful, terrifying midlife reckoning:

Feel the fear.

Let the grief of what you thought your life would look like pour through you.

And then? Let yourself remember who the hell you are.

You are not dying today. You are not done building.

You are not unlovable because your life doesn't look like a Lifetime movie.

You are not alone if you have even one person who sees you fully and says, "Still here."

Love might not arrive in the form you planned. But babe, you are love.

And that means you're already home.

Built from fire and rooted in truth,

—Angela

Real Girls Reflection:
How to embrace solitude.

What actually happens when you lean into the quiet instead of running from it? When you're asked to imagine life without kids or a partner, by choice or circumstance, your first thought might be fear: "Am I going to die alone?"

But sit in it. Feel the loneliness, the grief, perhaps the rage. Then breathe, because from that space, there's brilliance. Liberation. The potential to build connection on your own terms. To see solo not as a deficiency, but as a fierce, full life.

Take Laurie Nowling, for example. Midlife hit her with heartbreak, and she stayed single for nine years. Not the glossy, "finding herself" montage kind of single. The kind with bad dates, more tears than she can count, lonely nights, and raw come-to-Jesus moments. But on the other side of that pain came clarity: who she was, what she wanted and what she'd never again settle for.

Only after meeting *that* version of herself did she meet Russ, a partner who was calm where she was fiery, safe without being boring, and someone who let her be fully herself (and she, him). That's the point: She didn't find freedom in him, she found it in herself first. He was just the bonus track.

That same clarity is what pushed Laurie to co-create *She-bang*, with her friend Dodie, building a space for women in perimenopause and midlife to give back to themselves, pivot when needed, and reclaim their power. Not because Laurie's an "expert" in reinvention, but because she lived it. She clawed her way through the mess, solo, and came out stronger.

That's what leaning into the quiet can give you. Not just survival, but the chance to finally tell the truth about what you want, what you need, and what you're never going to tolerate again.

Find your people, love them loudly.

True community isn't just bloodlines and Sunday dinners with matching napkin rings.

It's the messy, makeshift village you stitch together out of your chosen family, group texts, porch wine nights, and the friends who'll fly across state lines just to help you pack up your life or your broken heart.

I've seen women build community from *nothing*.

From scratch. From grief. From bravery. From long-ass roads that did not lead to white-picket-fence endings.

One of my closest friends never had kids by choice and built a life so rich with connection it makes most suburban carpool moms seem emotionally bankrupt. She's got nieces and nephews she's helped raise, a crew so tight they finish each other's meltdowns, and friendships that have weathered more storms than most marriages. She's become everyone's emergency contact. That's legacy.

Another friend partnered into a family late—stepkids, exes, chaos, and all—and still managed to carve out space for real love. Not the rom-com kind. The hard, hilarious, soul-growing kind that takes therapy, grace, and a second fridge for the blended family snacks.

I've heard from single women who co-bought property and built co-housing communities where each person has their own space, but nobody feels alone when the lights go out. I've seen aunties and besties raise babies together. Women who've turned group chats into lifelines. Monthly potlucks into sacred rituals. Friendships into faith.

That is real community. It's radical. It's resilient. It's women saying: "If the world didn't give us the village, we'll build the thing ourselves—with snacks, boundaries, and a shared Hulu login."

As for me? I've got a long-distance love, a fused family of seven kids, and a girlfriend who FaceTimes me just to remind me to check my chin hairs. I've learned that real belonging doesn't come from DNA. It comes from showing up, again and again.

Final Takeaway

So, what will I borrow from these fierce, glorious women?

- I'll borrow the bravery of building bonds that *are not* defined by Hallmark.
- I'll borrow the freedom of saying, "These are my people, no approval required."
- I'll borrow the blueprint of connection that's transformative, not transactional.

Because community, at its core, is a rebellion. A refusal to be alone in the chaos. A sacred, chaotic, magnificent middle finger to the idea that family only counts if it shares your last name.

If that's not power, I don't know what is.

CHAPTER 14

The Real Girls Manifesto

"As long as I can, I will. Nothing—not doubt, fear, or confusion—is going to stop me."

—Kimberly Sheridan, PhD & Life Coach

Unlearning is sometimes harder than learning. It often means shedding decades of scripts we were handed about love, bodies, power and who we're "supposed" to be. You've heard my stories, the stories from other Real Girls, and the raw truths and wisdom from experts who know this terrain. Now it's time to ask: What do we carry forward, and what do we finally leave behind?

Here are my answers:

I unlearned that smaller is better.
That silence is graceful.
That sex is something I owe.
That grief is something to hide.
That my worth is tied to youth, thinness, or whether someone calls me "Mom."

I unlearned the gospel of bouncing back.
The myth of being "low maintenance."

The need to be liked in every goddamn room.
That friendship is forever.
That being tired means I'm lazy.
That being angry means I'm wrong.
That my aging body is a problem to solve.

I unlearned the thong.
(God bless her, she had her season, but she is Satan's shoelace now.)

I unlearned that blood makes family.
That motherhood is the only legacy.
That love must look a certain way,
and so must I.

I unlearned self-abandonment in the name of being "nice."
I unlearned shapeshifting.
Apologizing.
Over-explaining.
Shrinking to fit.

And in the space where all that used to live?

I learned that peace is not passive.
That rest is not weakness.
That saying "no" is holy.
That I can throw my back out picking up a sock
and *still* be a goddess in a bikini.

I learned that beauty moves.
That my body is a truth-teller,
a battlefield, a prayer.

That I'm no one's cup of tea,
but I'm my own favorite shot of whiskey.

I learned that midlife isn't the end.
It's the *unveiling*.

What broke open?
Everything I pretended didn't hurt.

What freed me?
Letting it.

What truth was hiding in plain sight?
That I was never broken.
Just buried.
And now, I'm back: louder, looser and lit the hell up.

Rest is not a fucking luxury:
Why I stopped earning my right to lie down.

Let me just say it straight: I used to believe that being tired meant I was lazy.

That if I didn't fold the laundry the second it dried—or better yet, if I asked a kid to fold it and then didn't put it away immediately—that I was somehow weak. Disorganized. Slipping.

I equated productivity with worth. Hustle with identity. I walked around like a one-woman stage production: caregiver, scheduler, peacekeeper, overachiever, snack supplier, emotional load-bearer, and hot damn if I didn't want a gold star for all of it. Except I didn't ask for one. I just wanted to be liked. Appreciated. Easy to love. Not difficult, not needy. Definitely not someone who *napped*.

Naps, back then, felt like failure. I'd lay down while the kids were tapping away on their iPads or watching a movie and instead of resting, I'd stew in guilt. One eye open. One ear tuned to chaos. One hand metaphorically writing the apology note for what I wasn't getting done.

I carried a massive stick called perfectionism and beat the living hell out of myself with it daily. I ran myself into the ground so things, me included, could look just right. I worked 14-hour days like they were a badge of honor.

And even now (retired, technically) I find myself agreeing to shit that exhausts me, because saying no still sometimes feels selfish. Like a chink in my "good mom" armor.

Case in point: Just recently I spent five and a half hours in the car shuttling my youngest kid (and his friends) to and from an amusement park that's only 30 miles away. Because traffic. Because favors. Because I still have a hard time not volunteering.

I wasn't even going on the trip, I was just the chauffeur. Just the giver, just the tired woman behind the wheel of a life that never stopped asking for more.

And then it hit me: Just because I *can* doesn't mean I *should*. Retirement doesn't mean endless availability. Being tired doesn't mean I've failed. Saying no doesn't mean I love them less. It means I finally love *me* more. Because it's not just physical exhaustion. I'm tired of how people treated me, tired of how *I* treated me. Tired of fake-smiling through the backhanded "compliments" and mean-ass jokes people make about my looks, my age, my body, my choices.

I'm tired of being taken for granted. Tired of feeling like shit and calling it normal. Tired of believing that asking for help made me weak, and that resting meant I hadn't earned it. But here's what I know now: Rest is not a reward. Rest is a right. Being tired is not lazy and being still is not indulgent. Saying "no" doesn't make me difficult, it makes me *dangerously self-possessed*.

That's the revolution, and the evolution.

Now? I don't apologize for needing space or lying down. For doing nothing or being too tired to fold laundry or give a shit about where someone's swim trunks went. Now I just say, "I'm tired," and I don't explain it away like a confession. I rest because my body asked. Because my brain needed it. Because I am not a machine.

Because after five decades of proving, pushing, and pleasing, I no longer need permission to stop.

Write Your Own Real Girls Manifesto

By the time we hit midlife, most of us have been shoved into reinvention by circumstance—divorce, layoffs, empty nests, health scares. Finance expert and podcaster Liz Svatek calls bullshit on waiting for life to shove you off the cliff: "Don't wait for life to force your evolution. Choose it. Shape it. Live it."

Reinvention doesn't have to be reactionary; it can be radical self-possession in motion. Her reminder is a rallying cry for this manifesto—an anthem for women reclaiming agency. Liz reminds us that reinvention isn't a crisis response, it's a conscious decision to become more of who we already are. Now, as an exercise in manifesting your own future:

Finish this sentence five times, without overthinking it: "Now that I'm in midlife, I will no longer _____."

Now finish it five more times, only reframed for what you will choose to do, fiercely and joyfully: "Now that I'm in midlife, I will fiercely, joyfully _____."

You now have 10 beautifully awesome sentences, choose one and write the full story of what that means in your life today. Here's how this looks once you've finished the exercise. I've filled in my own examples:

Now that I'm in midlife, I will no longer:

1. *Apologize for taking up space, making noise or needing rest.*
2. *Pretend I'm fine when I'm bleeding on the inside.*
3. *Squeeze into uncomfortable clothes, conversations or roles just to make others more comfortable.*
4. *Chase approval like it's currency.*
5. *Stay quiet to keep the peace when my truth is burning in my throat.*

Now that I'm in midlife, I will fiercely, joyfully:

1. *Say no without a single ounce of guilt.*
2. *Wear what feels good, even if it's labeled "shapeless" by some 30-year-old stylist.*
3. *Laugh so hard I pee (because, real talk, I am going to pee anyway).*
4. *Write the stories I was too scared to tell when I cared too much what others thought.*
5. *Show up fully, messy, wise, wrinkled, glorious, as myself.*

And here's the one I'm living out loud every single day:

"Now that I'm in midlife, I will no longer stay quiet to keep the peace when my truth is burning in my throat. Because I've done it. I've swallowed my truth at dinner tables, in boardrooms, in bedrooms. I've let people mistake my silence for agreement, let their assumptions shape the room while I shrunk to fit inside it.

I learned young that being 'too much' was dangerous. So, I edited. Smiled. Smoothed things over. Took pride in being palatable. Polite. Professional. Even when it made me ache. But that woman? She's gone.

She left quietly, the way she lived.

And in her place stands someone who won't trade peace with herself for the approval of people who wouldn't bleed for her.

Now? I speak. Even if my voice trembles.

I name the hard things: grief, resentment, desire, rage, boundaries.

I name my wants. My wounds. My worth.

I've learned that truth-telling is holy. That peace isn't the absence of conflict, it's the presence of alignment. And I won't go another year, another hour, another minute pretending I'm fine to make someone else more comfortable.

So, I speak. For me. For the woman I was.

For every woman still biting her tongue.

And for the ones coming next, so they don't wait until midlife to know that their voice was never too much...

It was always the whole damn fire."

What women questioning everything in midlife should know about surviving the next decade without apologies.

If a woman 10 years younger than me—tired, raw, doubting her worth—were to pick up this book and pop it open in the corner of some slightly-dusty downtown bookstore, I hope it would hit her like a permission slip dipped in gasoline.

Are you that person, dear reader? If so, I want you to know this:

You are not too much.

You are not behind.

You are not broken.

You are not fucking invisible.

And you are not required to set yourself on fire to keep everyone else warm.

You can stop earning your rest. You can stop chasing "better" like it's some holy destination. You can stop twisting yourself into palatable shapes for people who still don't fucking see you.

This book is not here to inspire you with bullshit mantras or clean-scrubbed middle-aged makeovers. It's here to walk you through the real, sagging, leaking, grieving, pissed-off, still-hot, still-hungry, still-holy truth of being a woman in the middle of life.

You want a takeaway? Here it is: Burn. The. Script.

All of it.

The one that says your body must bounce back. The one that says your worth is in what you produce. The one that says your value depends on how easy you are to love.

Own your mess. Feel your grief. Say no without a single fucking explanation.

Take the nap.

Buy the Spanx or toss them, whatever makes you feel most *you*. Touch your body like it belongs to you, because it does. And when someone calls you "brave" for being real, don't shrink. *Snarl*.

This chapter of life is not about fading. It's about rising. And if all you can do today is cry in the car, leave the laundry, and eat crackers in bed, you're still worthy as hell. So go ahead and spark.

Break free.

That's how the light gets in. And girl, you are the flame.

Here's my Real Girls pledge (no matter how scary it might seem):

I will not shrink myself: not for comfort, not for approval, not to be less intimidating, easier to love or more "palatable." Even when it terrifies me, I will take up space, speak too loudly, want too much, and own every messy, magic-fueled part of who I am becoming.

Yeah, it scares the shit out of me. Because for decades I played the role: good girl, good wife, good mom, good worker bee. I edited myself in rooms where I should've roared and soared. I downplayed my intelligence, softened my opinions, laughed off my trauma, and swallowed my worth like it was a vitamin I hadn't earned yet.

But not anymore.

Now, I walk into rooms unshrunk. With crow's feet, battle scars, hormone swings, and dreams so big they don't fit into a filing cabinet. I say no without explanation. I rest without guilt. I choose me, first, loud, and without a permission slip.

This is what it means to live the manifesto, to show up scared but still fucking standing. To risk being "too much" in a world that told you your whole life to be less. To claim joy, rage, rest, pleasure, and power as your birthright.

So here I am, voice shaking, knees wobbling, and still saying it louder every single day—I'm not here to fit in. I'm here to set it on fire.

Let the scared parts shake. I've got her now.

Tying it all together with a single truth.

The golden thread running through this entire book is that I never stopped showing up, even when I didn't recognize the woman staring back at me in the mirror. Even when my body betrayed me. Even when I was so tired I could cry from the effort of pretending I was OK.

Writing this book split me wide open. Every story, every scar, every chapter where I told the truth (finally), fully-stitched me back together in ways I didn't know I needed. I started off thinking I was writing all of this for other women, but the truth is, I wrote my way back to *me*.

I faced the grief I'd buried. I grieved the girl who tried so hard to earn her place. I grieved the woman who hustled for love, for worth, for peace, and still felt like it wasn't enough. And then I made peace with her.

I held her hand. I told her: *You don't have to try so hard anymore.*

This book taught me that power isn't something you wait to be handed. You take it back, piece by piece, breath by breath, boundary by boundary. It taught me that aging isn't a decline, it's a fucking awakening. That everything I thought made me "too much" is actually what makes me unstoppable.

And here's what I believe now, with marrow-deep certainty: We are never past our prime. We are in it. Right here, right now. With soft bellies and loud voices, stretch marks and sharper instincts. With grief still tucked in our pockets and joy waiting in our next brave decision.

This isn't just a book. It's a reckoning. And I am not the same woman who started writing it.

I'm more honest.

More unapologetic.

More me than I've ever been.

So, if you're reading this, flipping through pages, wondering if it's too late to come home to yourself, let me be the one who reaches back and says: It's not too late, not even close. And when you forget, read it again.

I wrote this book for both of us, for all of us.

ACKNOWLEDGEMENTS

This book isn't just mine. It's stitched together from the voices, stories, and fire of hundreds of women and extraordinary experts. To all of you who gave me your words, your time, and your truth—thank you. You made this real.

To the writers Jen Sincero and Cheryl Strayed, whose words reminded me that women can do anything, build anything, become anything— and that the world is better when we do.

A huge thank you to Carrie Drew, who has been both my right hand, and my left. The one who believed when I didn't, who poured her heart and soul into me and into this book, and who stood steady every single step of the way. And to Brad Drew, who mapped the moves across every page and always saw ten steps ahead—thank you for holding the line and helping bring it to life when it mattered most.

To the Real Girls Guide community—every single one of you who's read, shared, commented, messaged, or whispered "same." You're the heart-beat of this movement.

Deep gratitude to my early readers, Leslie A, Sarah G, and Sarah H, for helping to sharpen the story, hold me accountable, and bring this to life with more clarity and heart; and to Nate Birt, whose guidance and steady support helped me power through the manuscript.

Last, but definitely not least, to my amazing bunch of ride-or-dies—including my lifer, Julie D—who've given me constant support and encouragement; my three boys who made me a mom and continue to show me, every day, what unconditional love and real pride look like; my brother Anthony and my sisters Amy and Allison; and my Aussie Man—plus the incredible crew of kids who came with him—thank you for loving me, for keeping me laughing when I needed it most, and for reminding me that family always shows up, in a thousand different ways.

EXPERTS, REFERENCES & SOURCES

Thank you to the individuals who contributed their expertise, perspective, and/or personal story. Your insight and generosity strengthened and grounded this work (in alphabetical order):

Cris Amato, MSN, APN, RNFA and founder of Grace Concierge; Dr. Nick Bach, PsyD, psychologist and marriage counselor; Charles Bauman, LMFT and therapist; Annette Benedetti, Sex & intimacy coach, host of *Talk Sex With Annette* (podcast); Nikoo Berenji, Partner at Berenji & Associates Family Law Attorneys; Kathy Boufford, Author and dedicated family attorney; Jacqui Burge, Wellness coach and founder of XO Jacqui; Michelle Cantrell, Licensed therapist and founder of The Center for Growth & Connection; Molly Carroll, Therapist and host of the *Cracking Open* podcast; Christine Dickson, Transformational mentor; Dr. Elizabeth Franze, Pelvic Floor Therapist & Sex Counselor; Holly Gedwed, LPC-Associate; Traci Griffin, Founder of Achieve Greatness Daily; Ross Hackerson, LMFT; Diane Heiler, Author of *A Widow's Fire: An Intimate Memoir of Heartbreak, Survival, and Moving On* (Independently Published, 2025); Danielle Jenkins, RN and founder of Fourth Avenue Aesthetics in South Australia; Ben Kiker, former Silicon Valley CMO and leadership mentor; Diane Lang, M.A., counselor, coach, author and speaker, has written several books, including *Mindfully Happy: Waking Up to Life*, among others; Lisa Martin,

Tech broadcaster, analyst and former host of theCUBE; Alexis McCray, Ed.S and LPC; Viviana McGovern, EMDR-certified therapist; Dr. Nivedita Nayak, Clinical psychologist; Laurie Nowling, Co-Founder of Shebang; Missy Toy Ozeas, Energy Healer, Intuitive Channel, and Creator of the Become a Money Magnet Workshop; Nicky Price, Transformation Therapist and Success Coach; Dr. Carol Queen, longtime sex educator and staff sexologist at Good Vibrations; Dr. Trina Read, Sexologist & author of *Sex Boot Camp* (Sensual Tastes Publishing, 2010; updated workbook 2024); Jenna Richardson, Certified Menopause Specialist, FDN-P and CEO of Princeton Integrated Health; Bronwyn Saglembeni, Founder of BRONWYN Communications, executive coach; Dr. Kimberly Sheridan, PhD and professor of Educational Psychology, and founder of Fueled By Soul; Dr. Noah St. John, Author and mindset coach ("mental chiropractor"), incl. *The Secret Code of Success* (HarperOne, 2009); Candice Suarez, Founder of Season of Flight; Liz Svatek, Podcaster and author of *Finding Your Diamonds: Heal the Girl and the Warrior Appears* (Independently Published, 2025); Sarah Wendell, Co-founder of Smart Bitches Trashy Books and co-author of *Beyond Heaving Bosoms* (Touchstone, 2009).

Some of the titles below are quoted directly, others informed the questions, tone, and perspective woven throughout this book (in alphabetical order):

Tiffany Aliche ("The Budgetnista"), *Get Good with Money* (Rodale Books, 2021); Alua Arthur, *Briefly Perfectly Human* (HarperOne/HarperCollins, 2024); Claire Bidwell-Smith, *Anxiety: The Missing Stage of Grief* (Da Capo Lifelong Books/Hachette, 2018); Brené Brown, *The Gifts of Imperfection* (Hazelden Publishing, 2010); Tess Brigham, *True You* (Archway Publishing, 2022); Dr. Thema Bryant, *Homecoming* (TarcherPerigee, 2022); Joseph Campbell, *The Hero with a Thousand Faces* (Pantheon Books, 1949); Dr. Shannon Chavez (cited for clinical expertise); Dr. Mary Claire Haver, *The Galveston Diet* (Rodale Books, 2023); Amanda Clayman (cited for financial therapy and behavior); James Clear, *Atomic Habits* (Avery, 2018); Heather Corinna, *What Fresh Hell Is This?* (Hachette Go, 2021); Marcia Drut-Davis, *Confessions of a Childfree Woman* (2013); Dr. Anne Duch (cited for pelvic health expertise); Maddy Dychtwald, *Ageless Aging* (Mayo Clinic Press, 2024); Sallie Krawcheck, *Own It* (Crown

Business, 2017); Julie Lythcott-Haims, *How to Raise an Adult* (Henry Holt, 2015); Dr. Emily Nagoski, *Come As You Are* (Simon & Schuster, 2015; rev. 2021); Vanessa Marin, *Sex Talks* (Simon Element, 2023); Utkala Maringanti (cited for clinical expertise); Davina McCall, *Menopausing* (HQ/ HarperCollins, 2022); Tara Mohr, *Playing Big* (Gotham Books, 2014); Anna Olsen (cited for coaching and media work); Pasqualina Perrig-Chiello (cited for academic work); Chanel Reynolds, *What Matters Most* (Harper Wave, 2019); Julia Samuel, *Grief Works* (Penguin Life, 2017); Sonya Renee Taylor, *The Body Is Not an Apology* (Berrett-Koehler, 2018; 2nd ed. 2021); Jacquette Timmons, *Financial Intimacy* (Chicago Review Press, 2009); Farnoosh Torabi, *When She Makes More* (Hudson Street Press, 2014); Lynne Twist, *The Soul of Money* (W.W. Norton, 2003); V (formerly Eve Ensler), *The Vagina Monologues* (Villard, 1998).

ABOUT THE AUTHOR

ANGELA BURK is an award-winning high-tech Marketing Leader, Author, and the voice behind Real Girls Guide to Midlife, a community reshaping how women step into midlife with radical self-possession. After three decades scaling companies from scrappy pre-IPO startups to global Fortune 500 giants, she left the C-suite to focus on consulting, writing, and telling the truth about what it really means to live on your own terms.

Her Substack and this book blend personal stories with hard-won insight and expert guidance, delivering real talk, sharp observations, and a voice women can relate to immediately.

Angela divides her time between the San Francisco Bay Area and Australia and is a mom to three boys and a stepmom to four more kids.

www.ingramcontent.com/pod-product-compliance
Lightning Source LLC
Chambersburg PA
CBHW020232130626
46549CB00005B/1852